AF478931

Salt n vinegar

Salt 'n vinegar
A - CHEW

Steidl

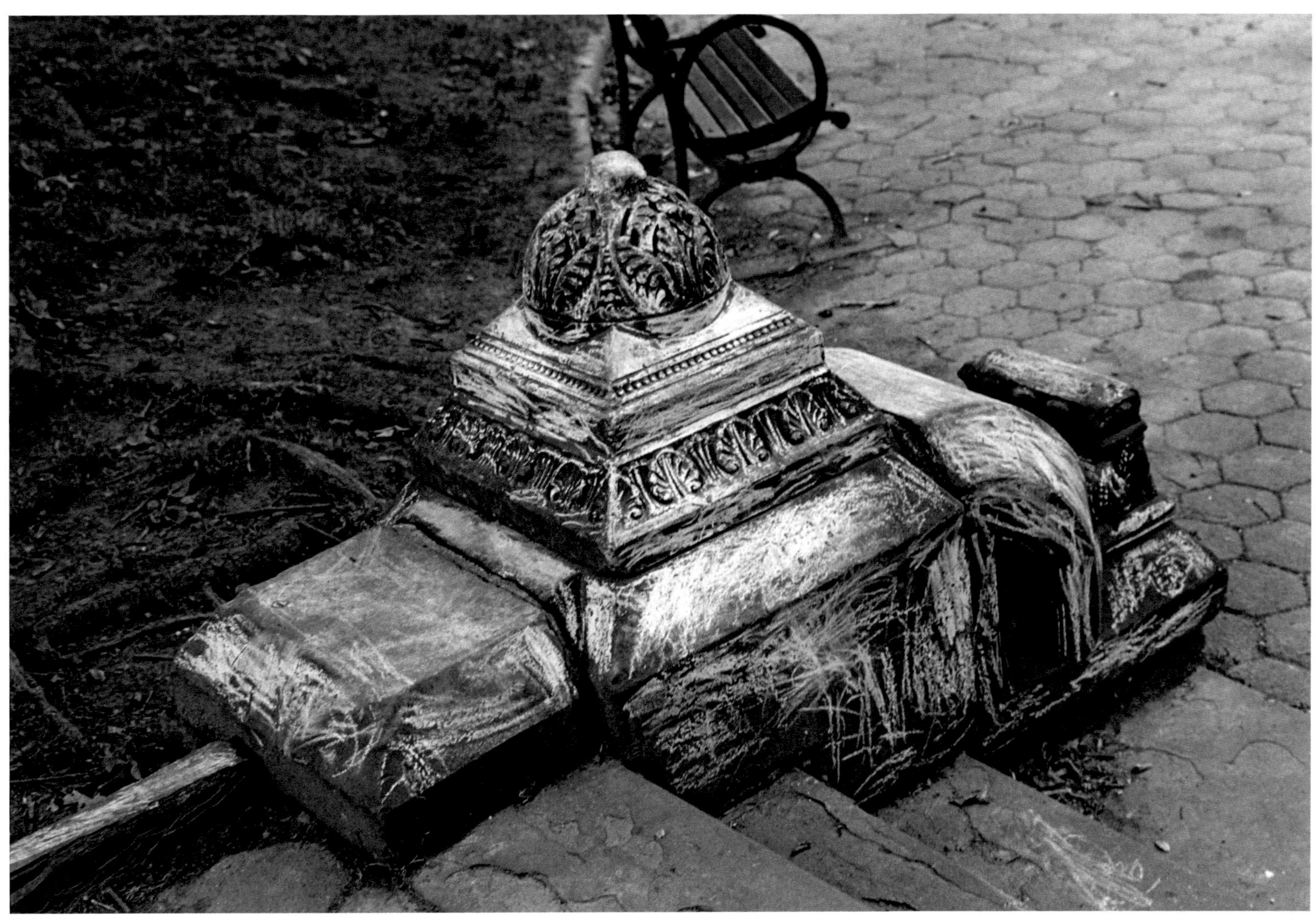

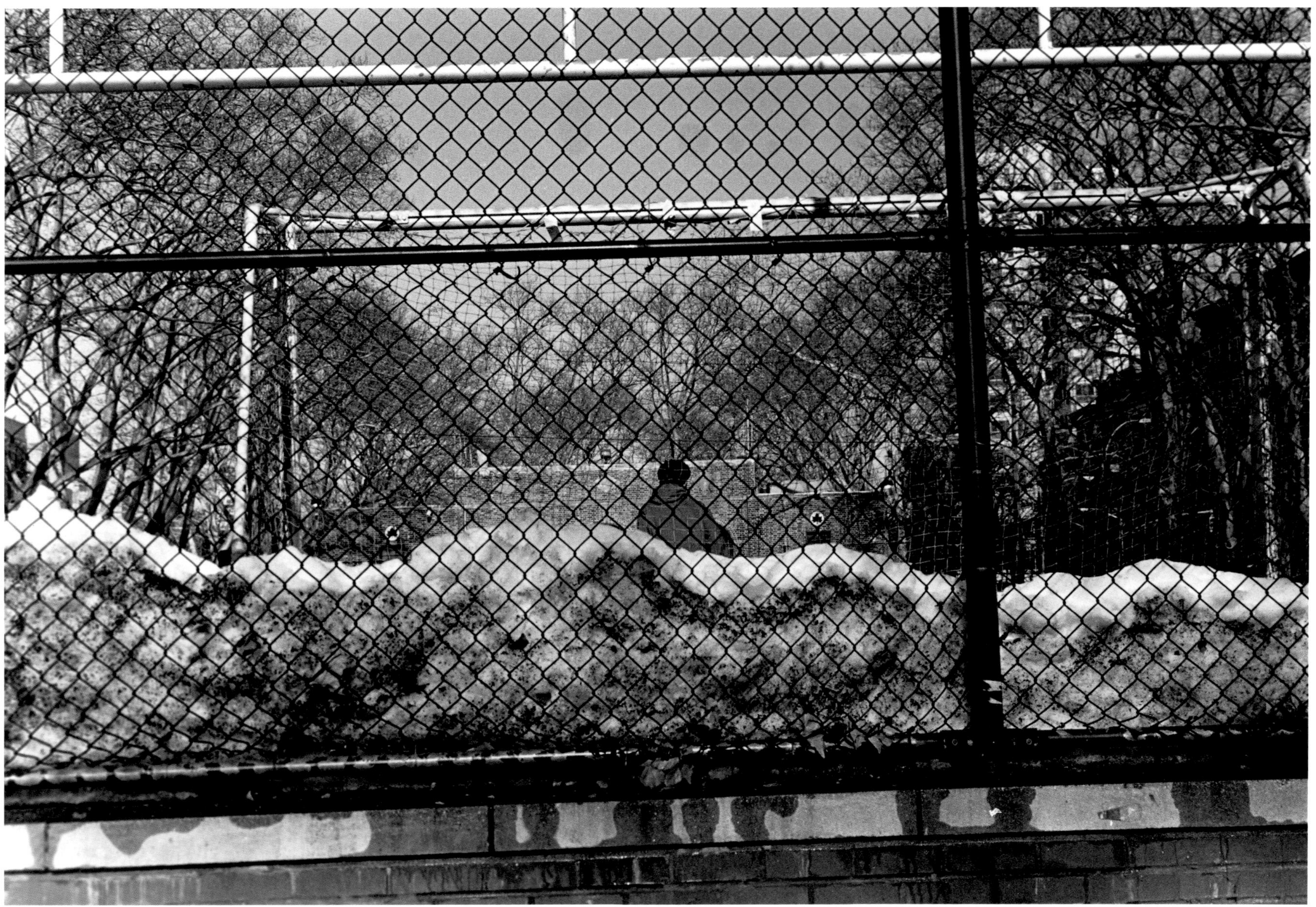

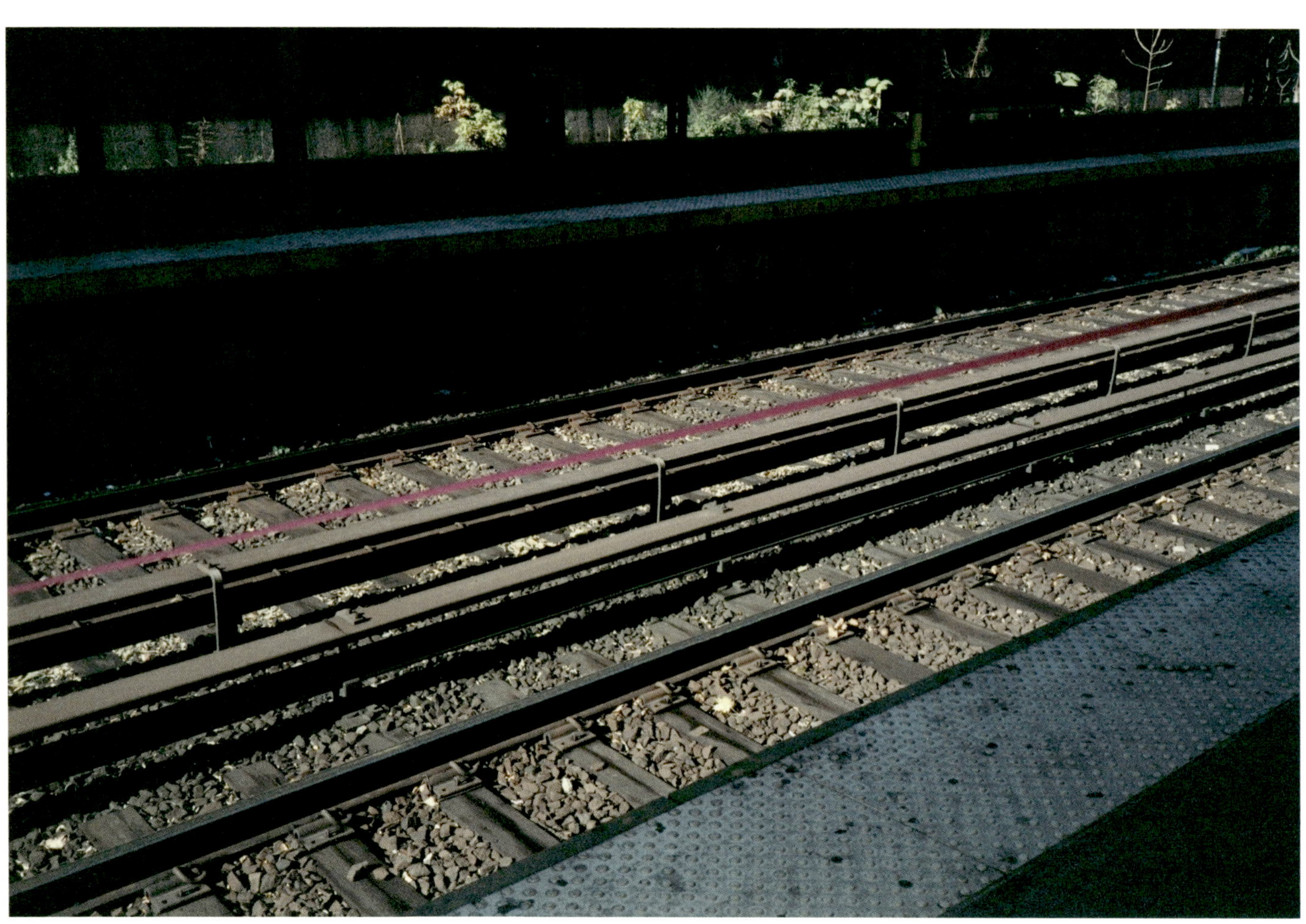

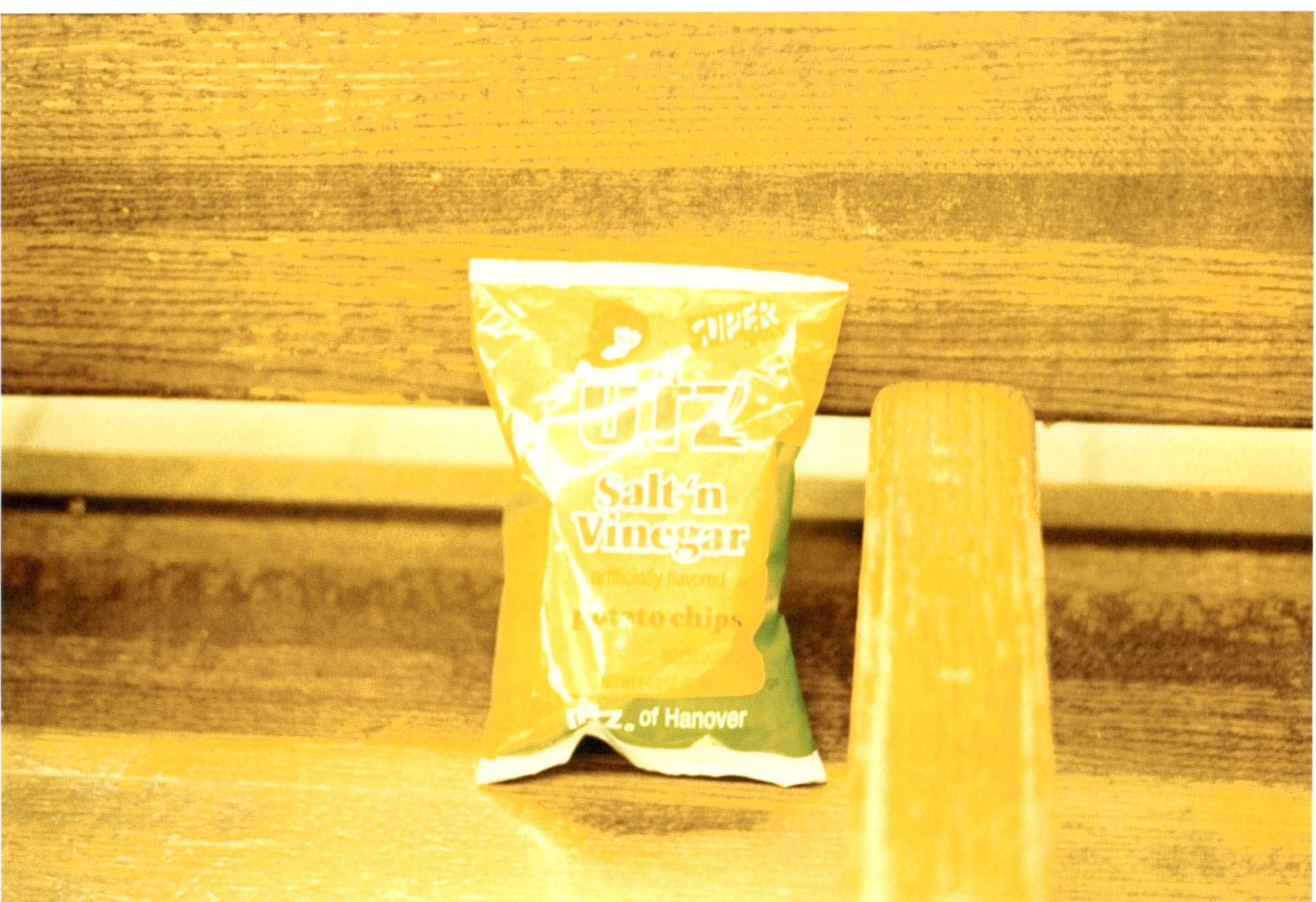
SUPER
Utz
Salt 'n
Vinegar
artificially flavored
potato chips
Utz. of Hanover

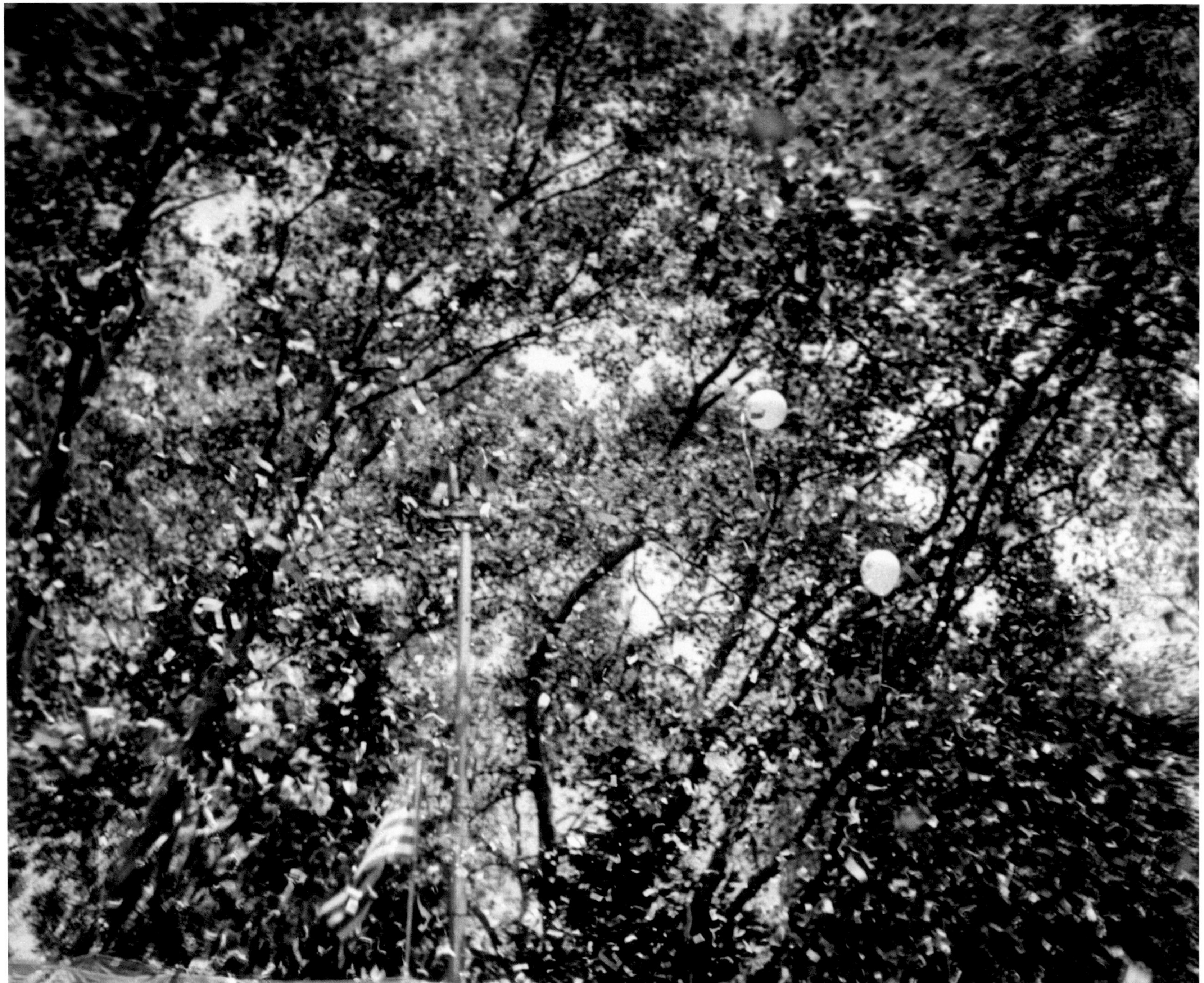

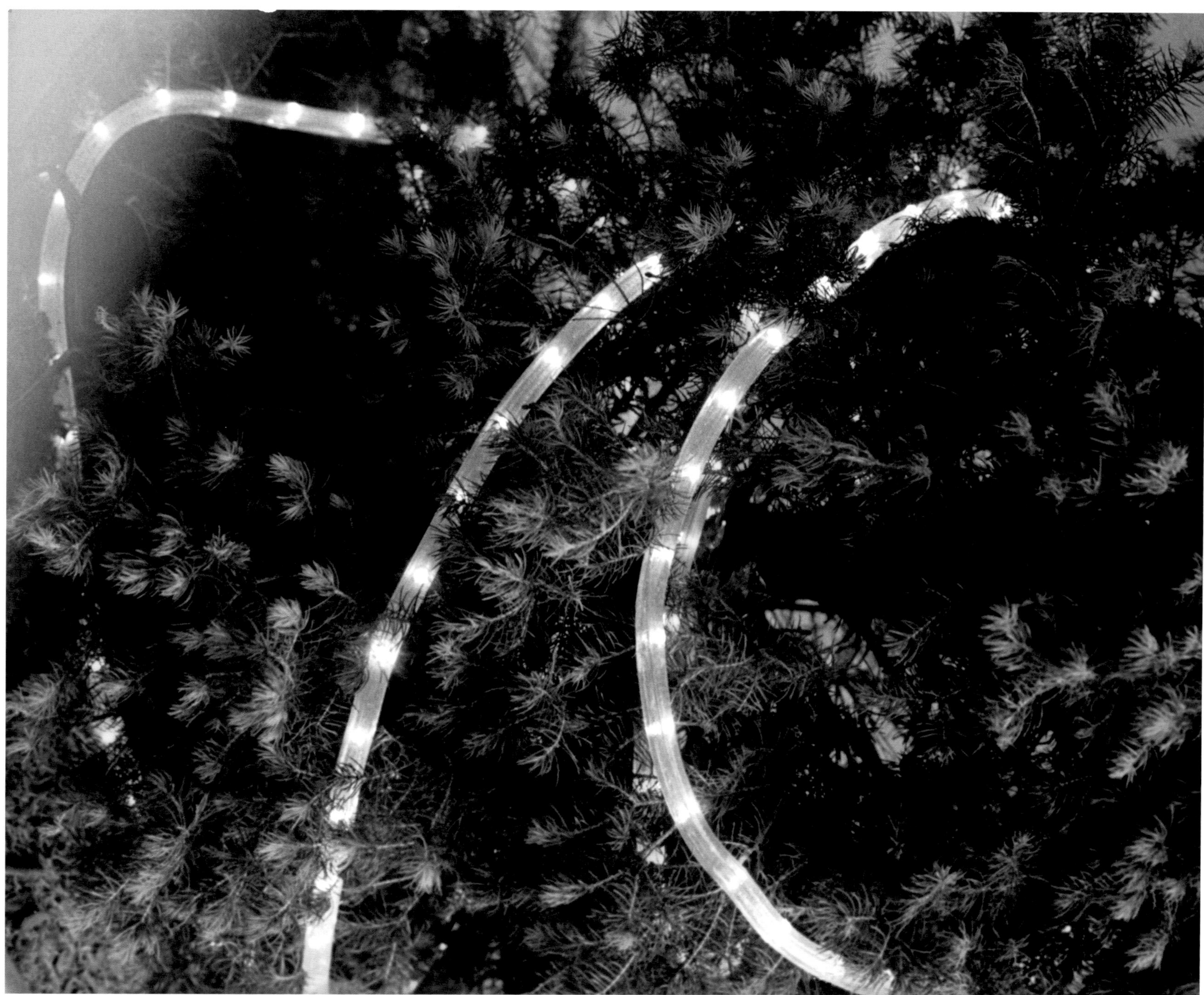

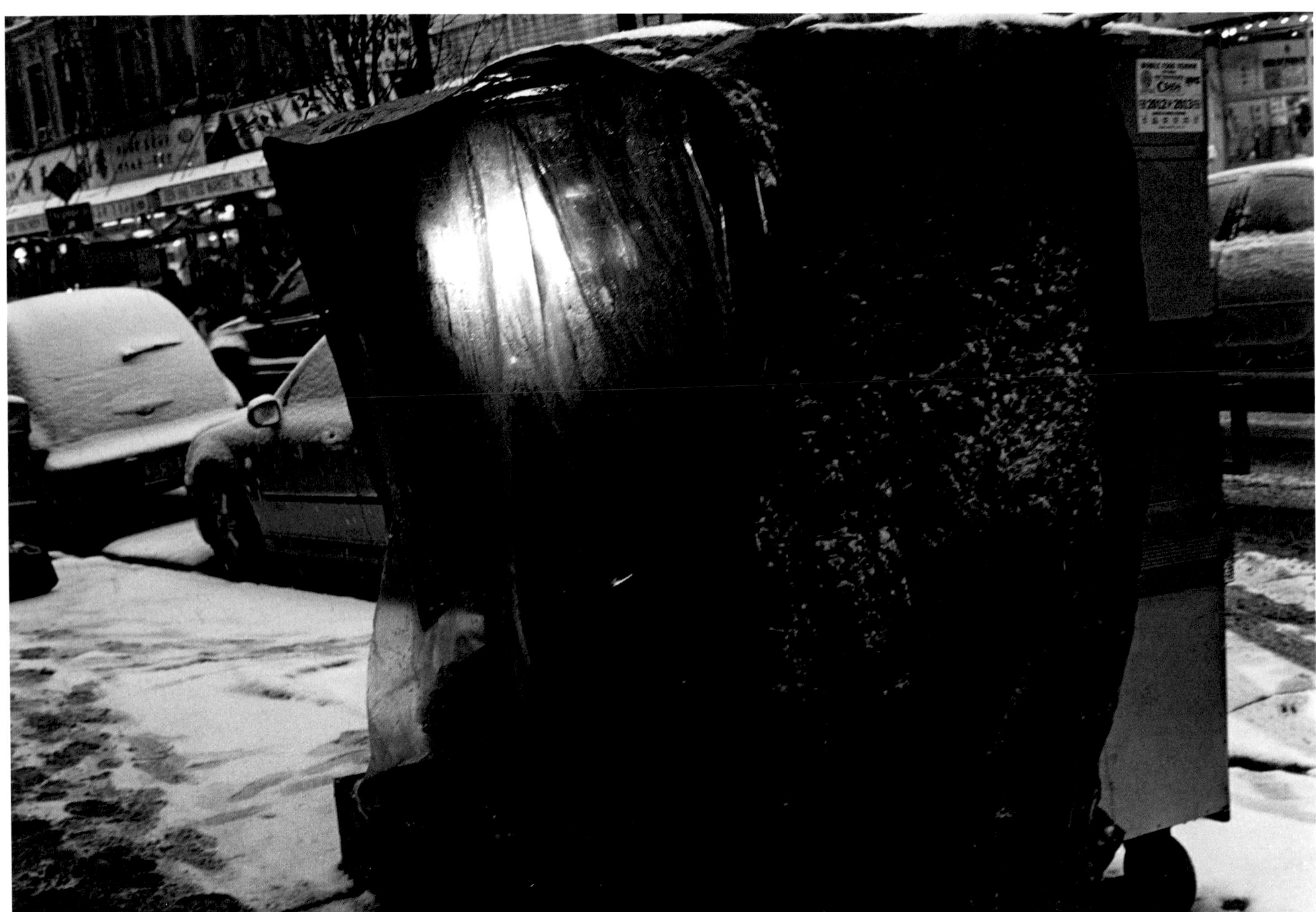

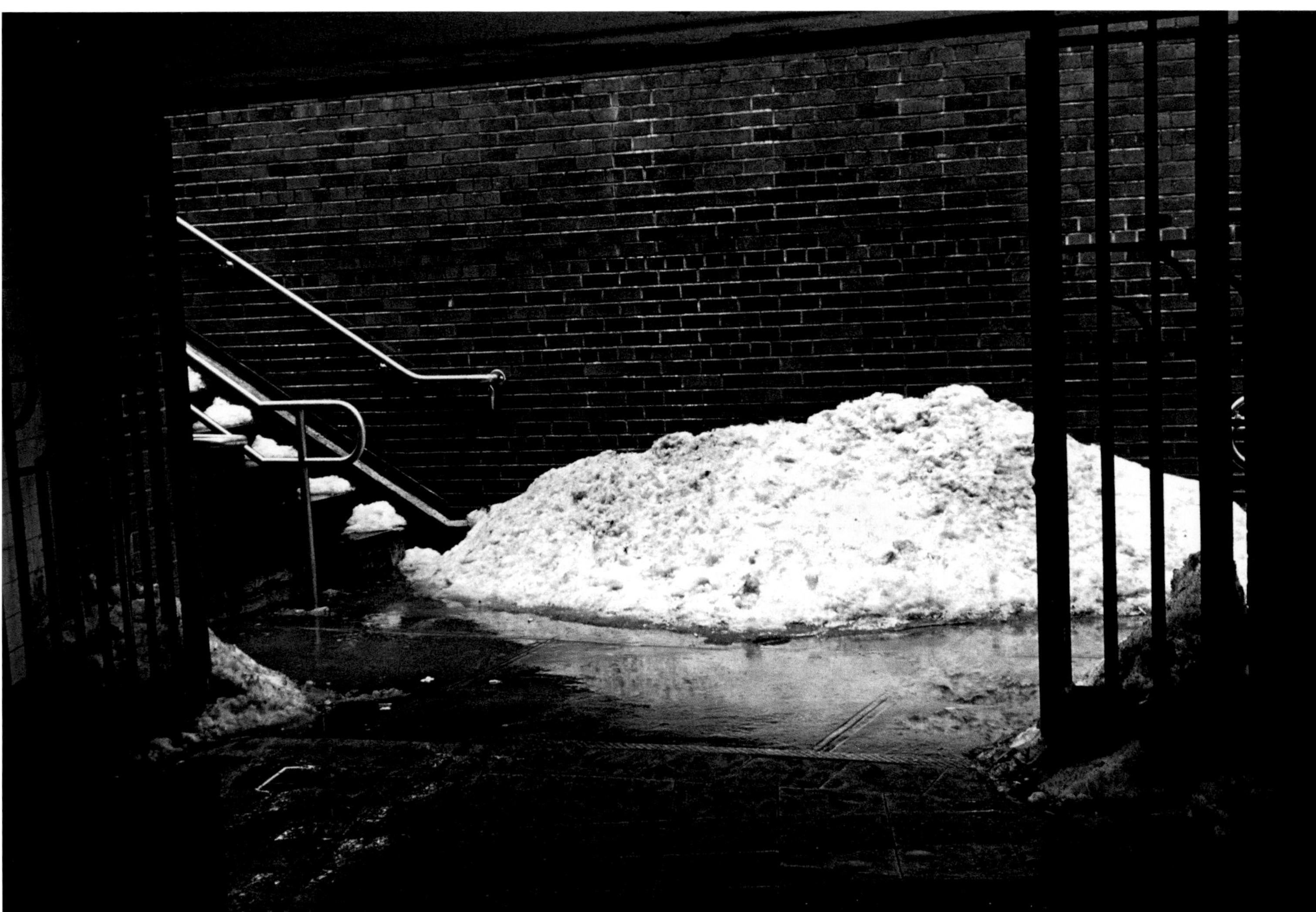

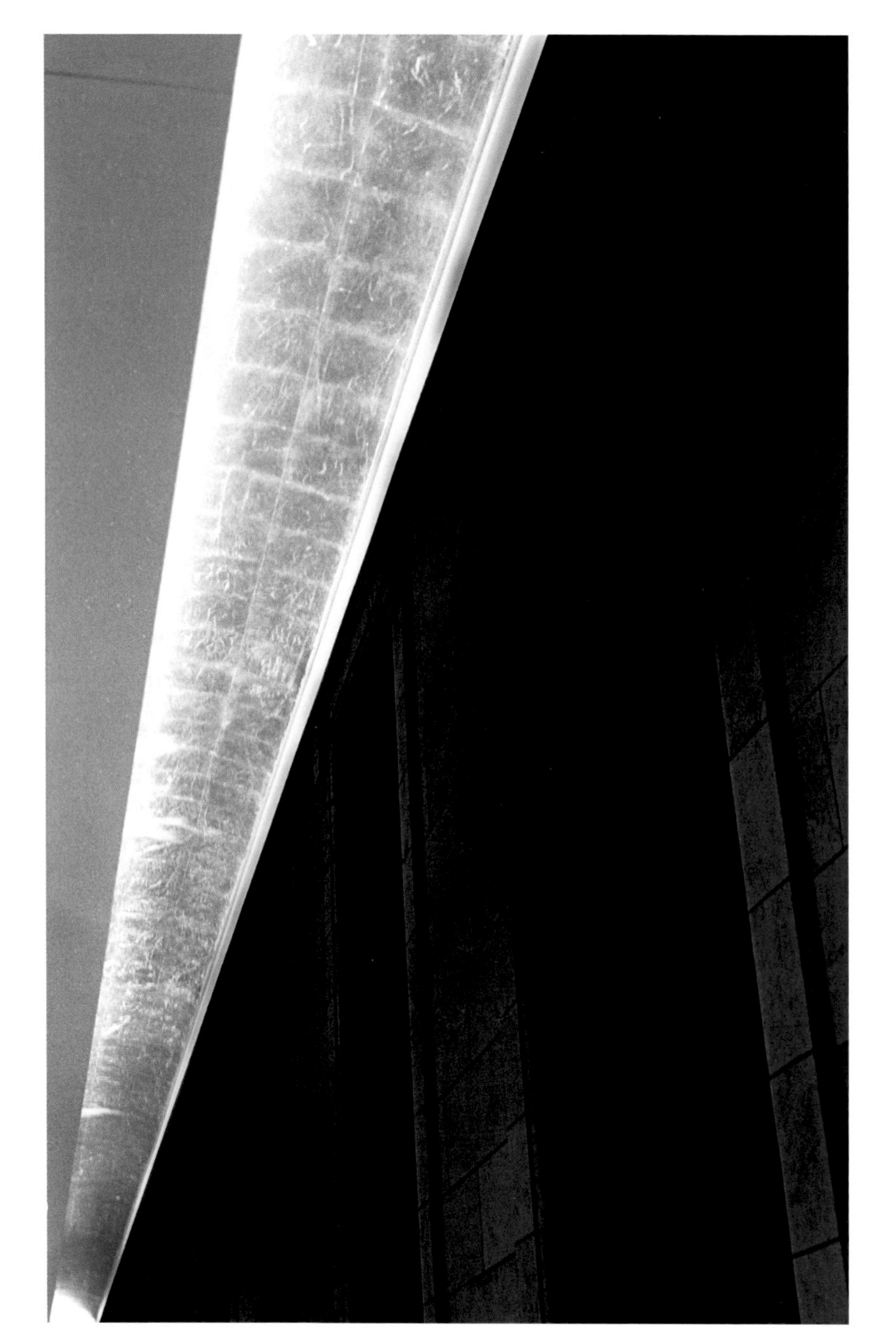

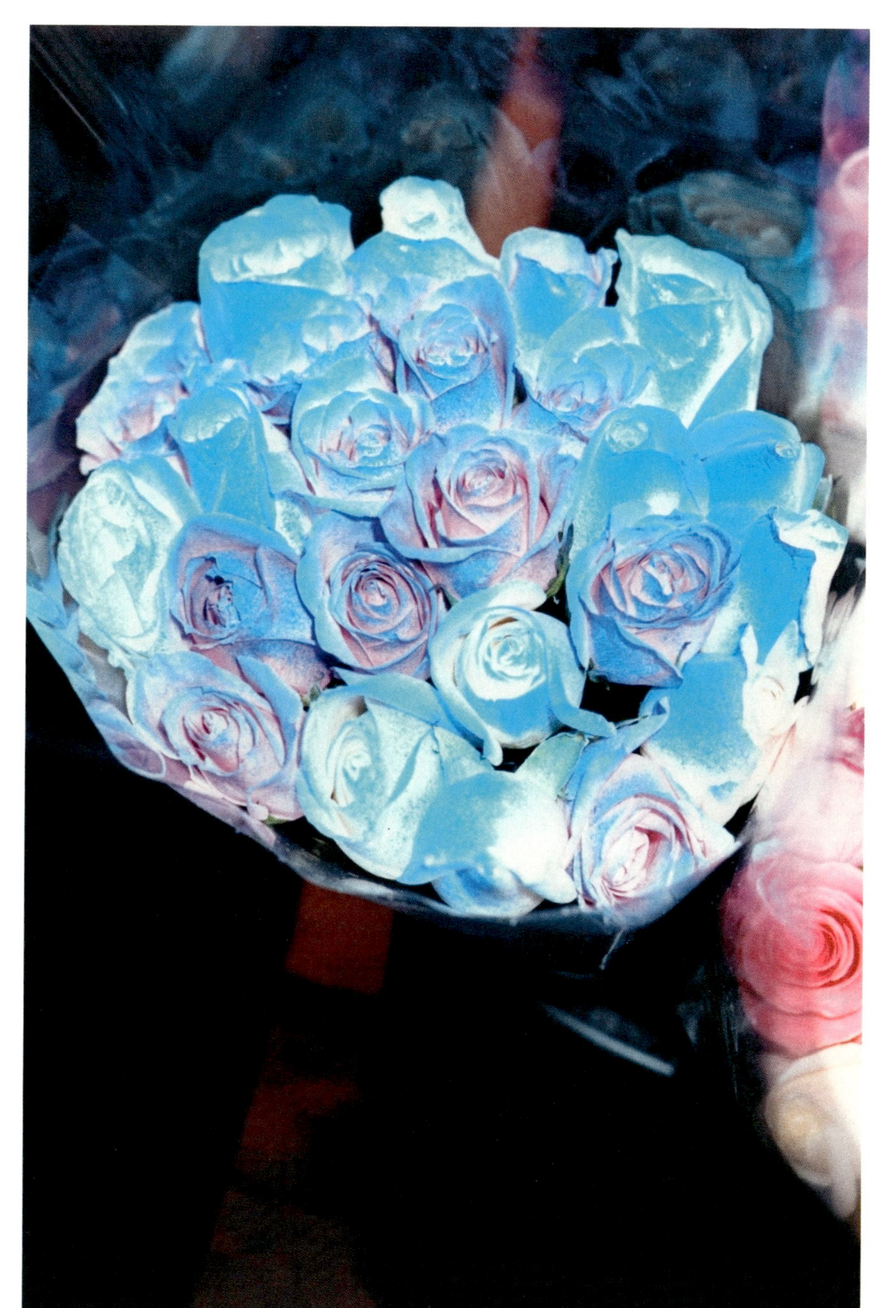

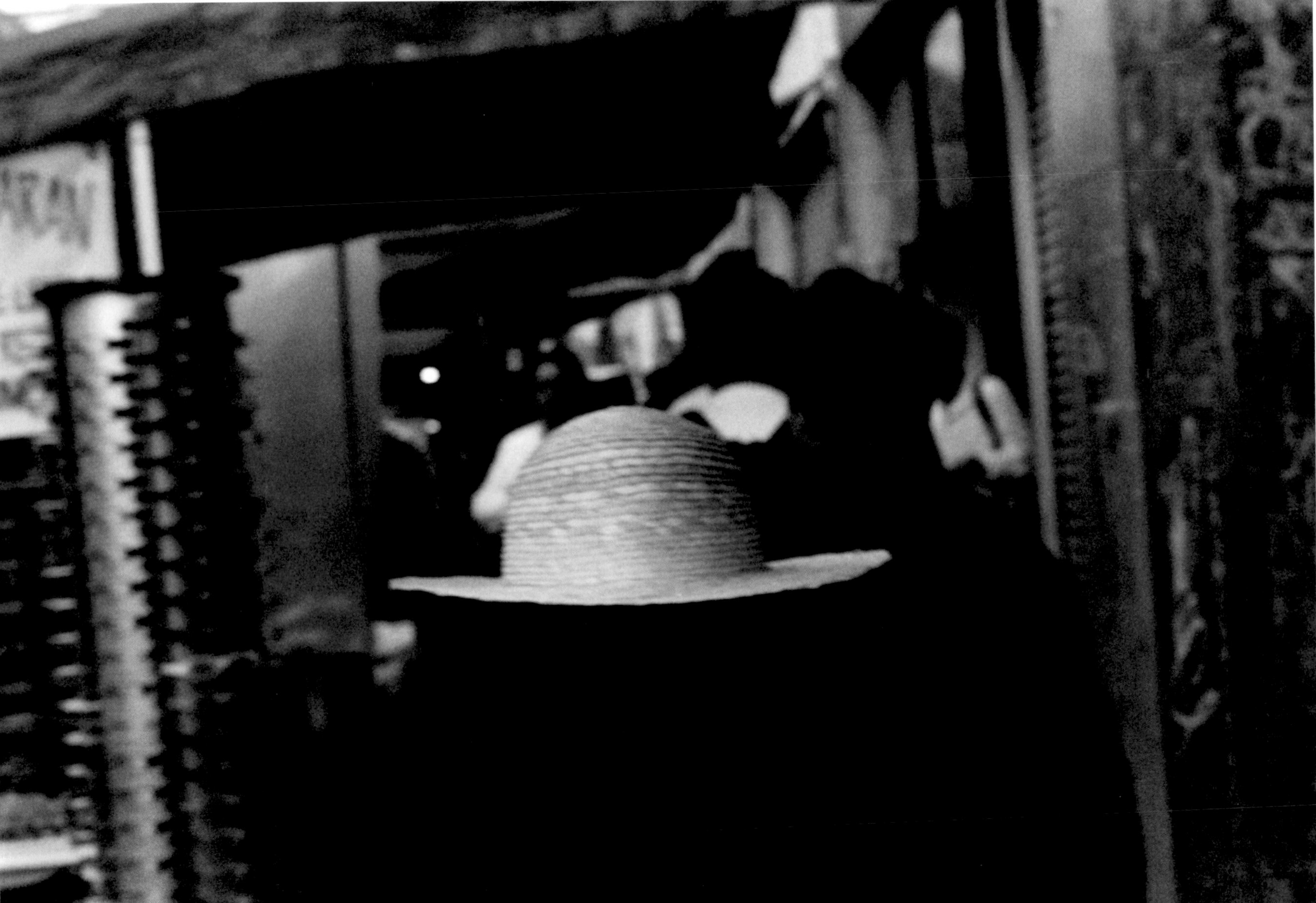

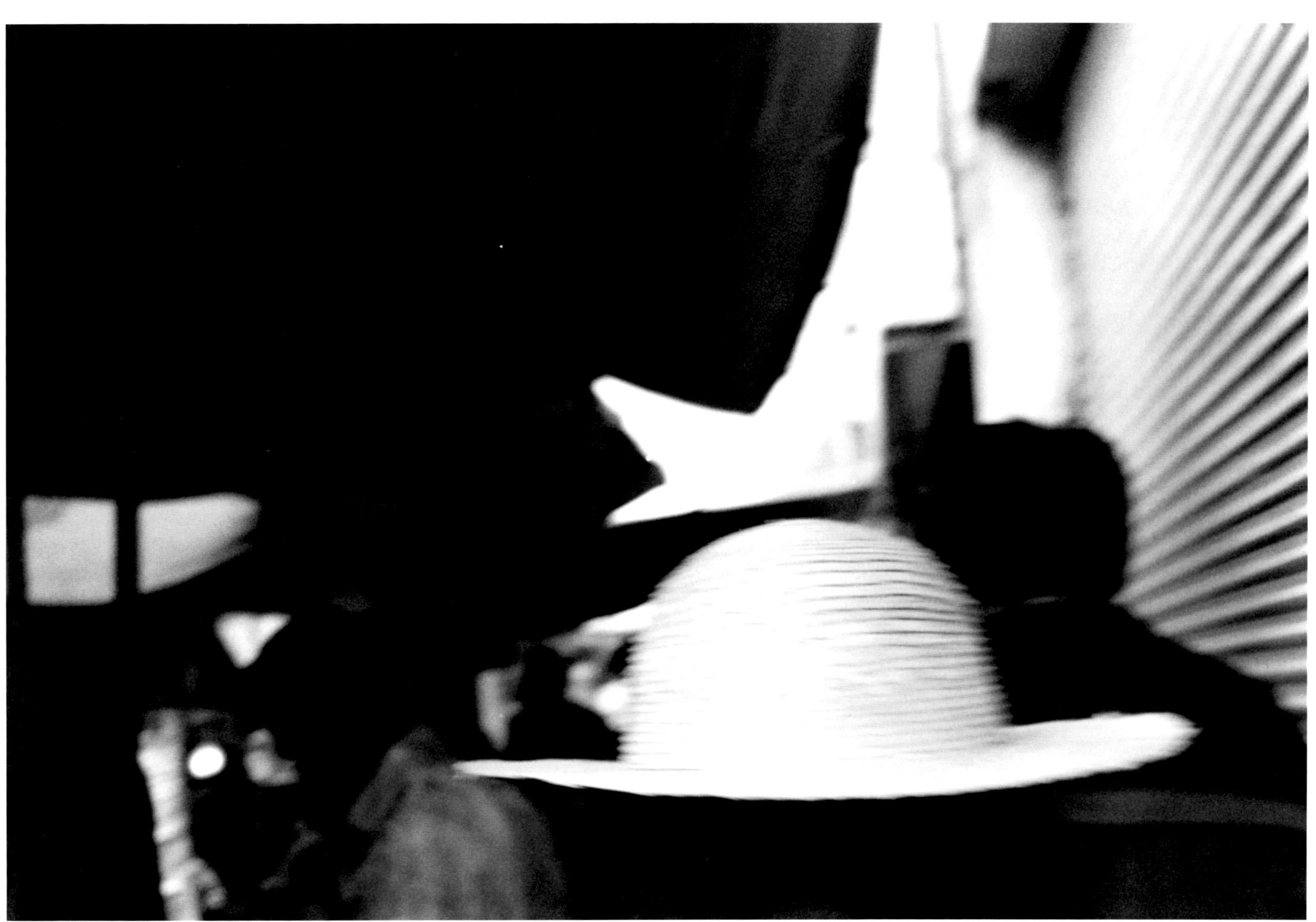

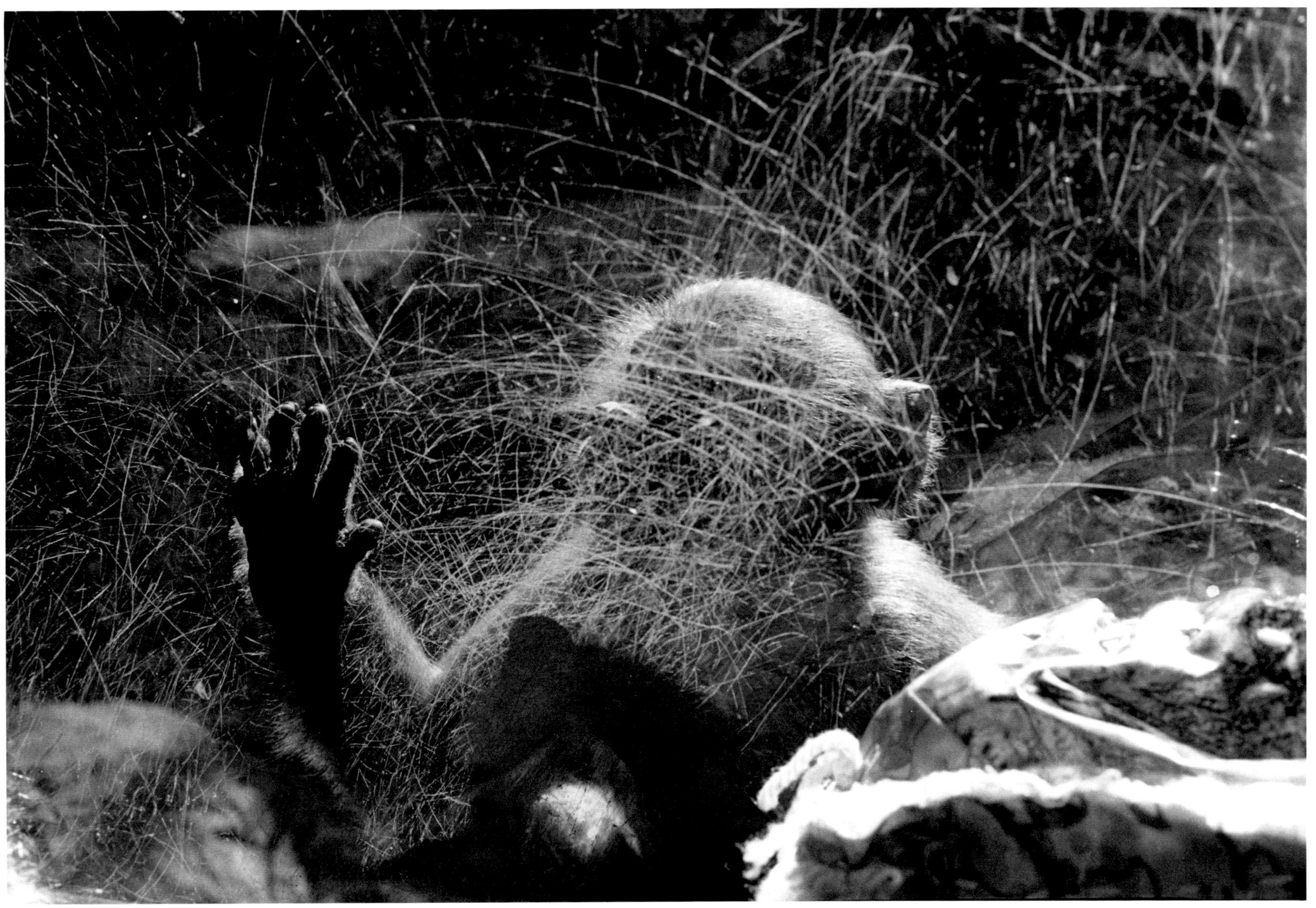

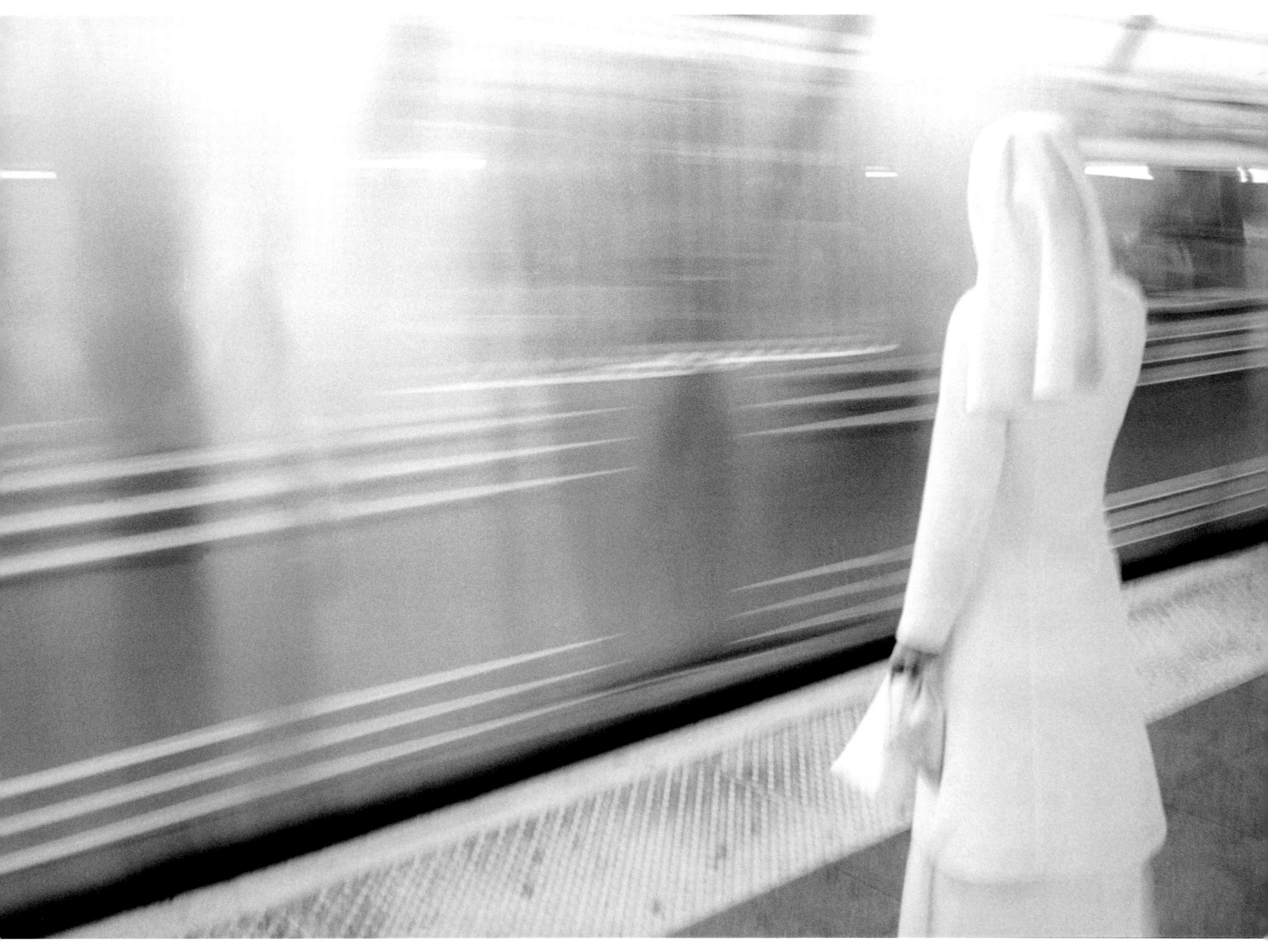

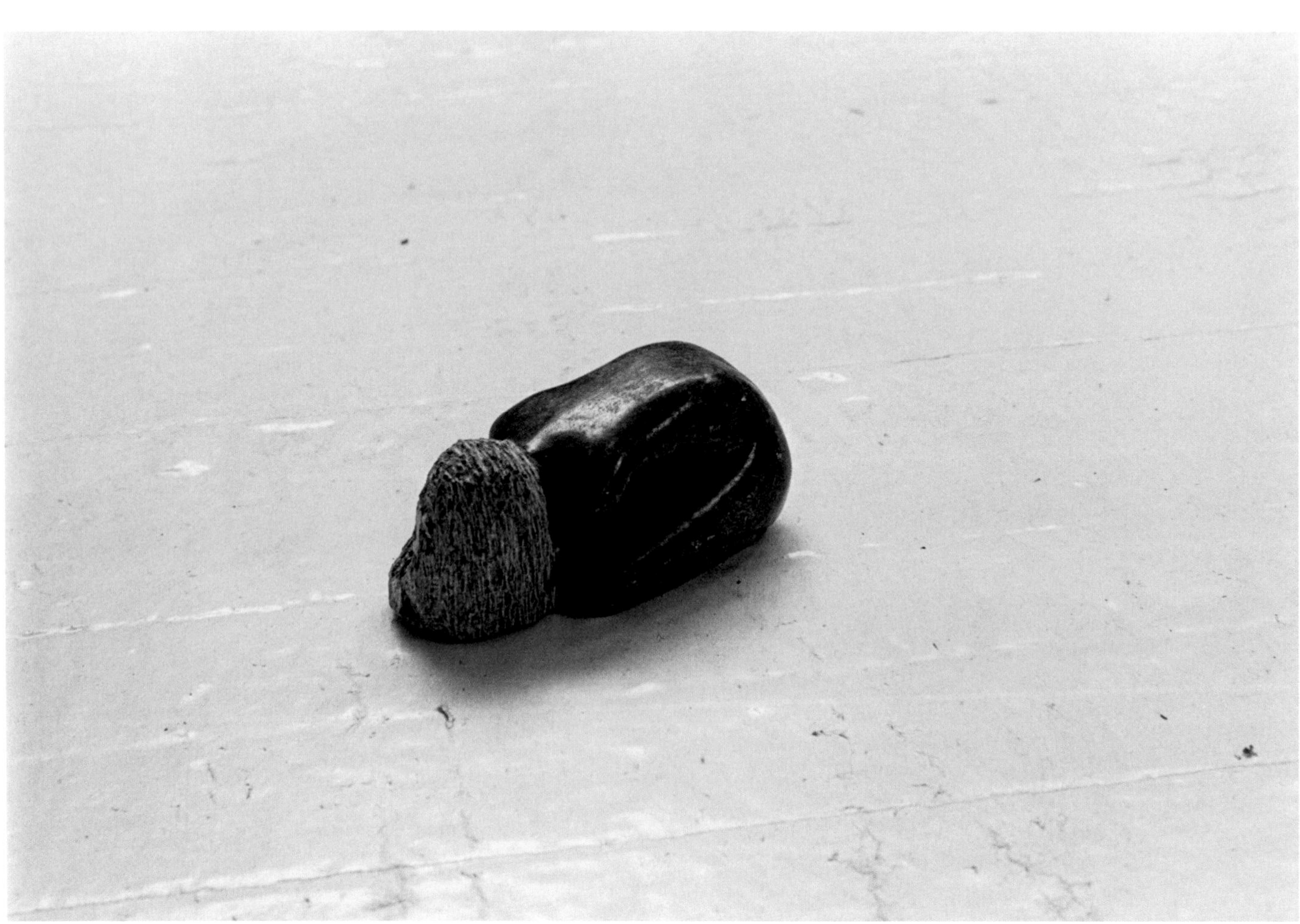

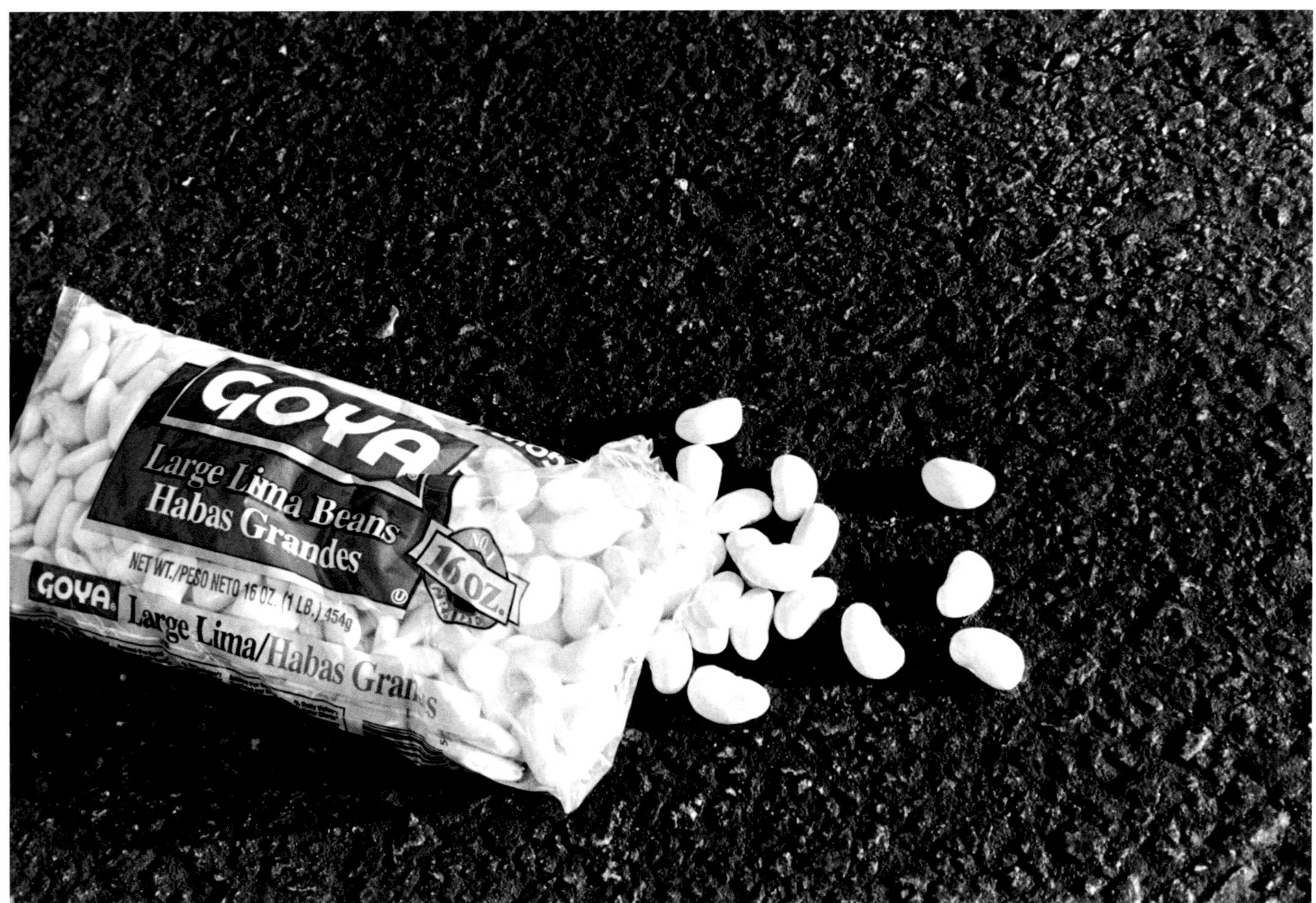
GOYA
Large Lima Beans
Habas Grandes
NET WT./PESO NETO 16 OZ. (1 LB.) 454g
16 OZ.
GOYA
Large Lima/Habas Grandes

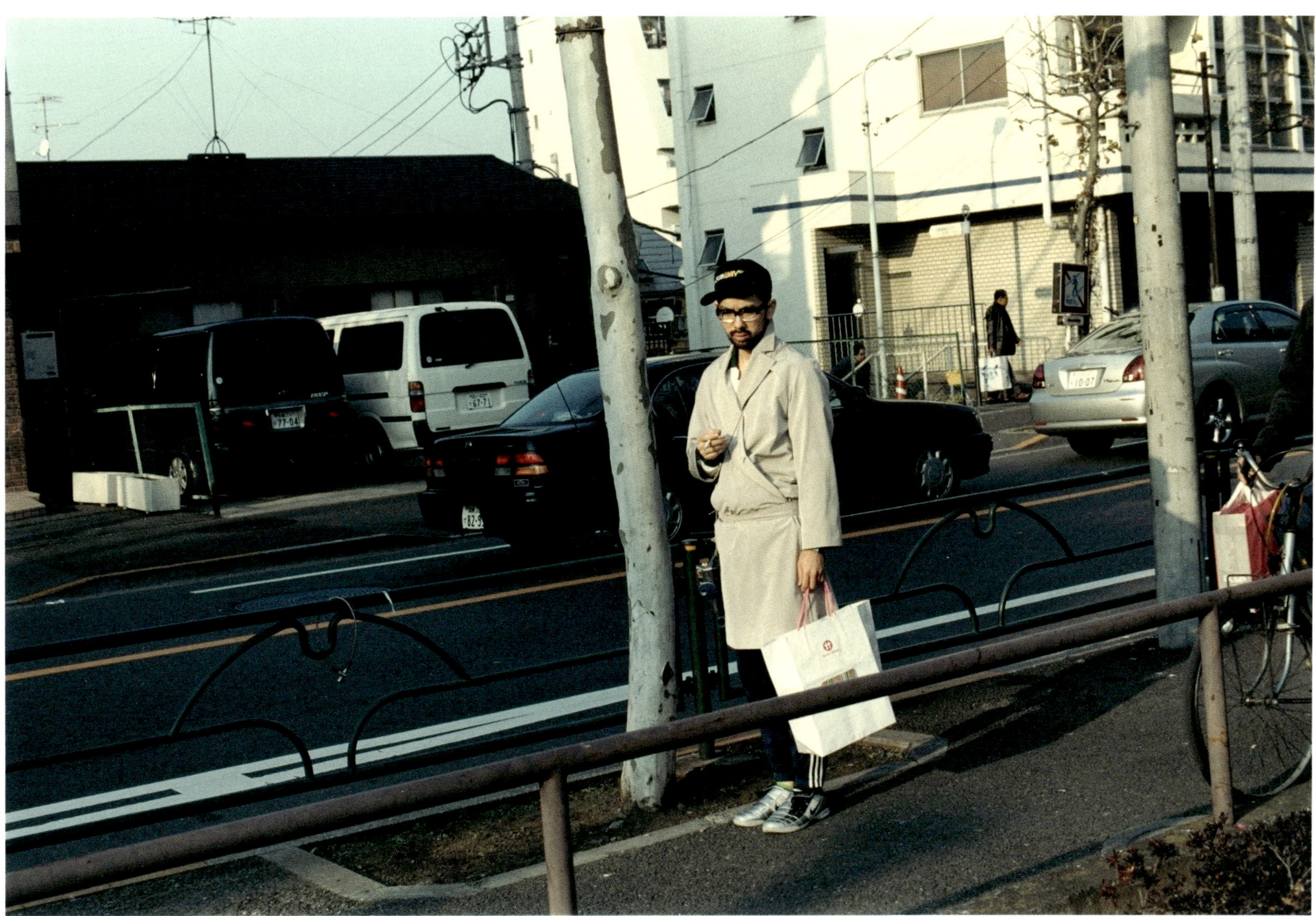

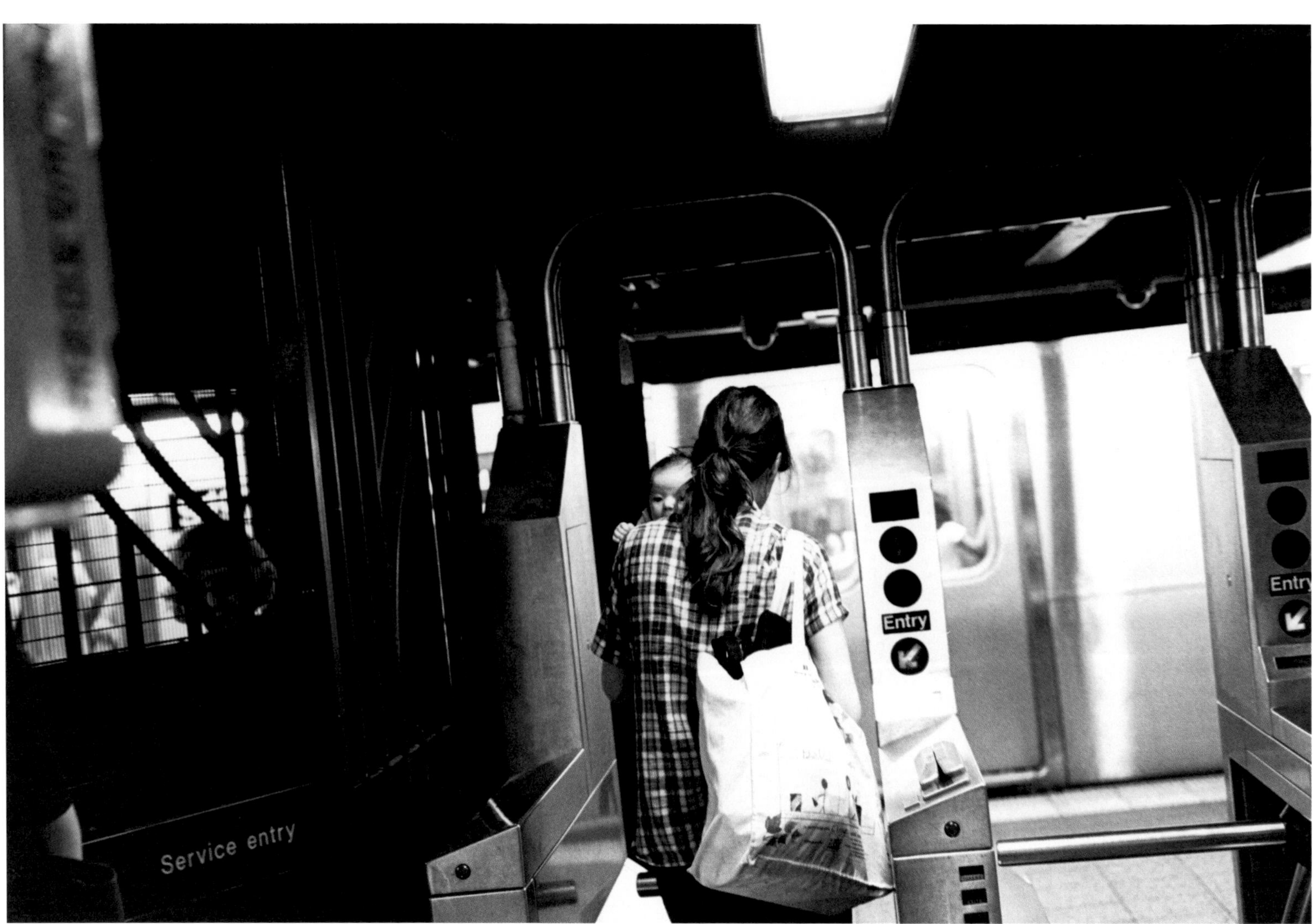

Service entry
Entry
Entry

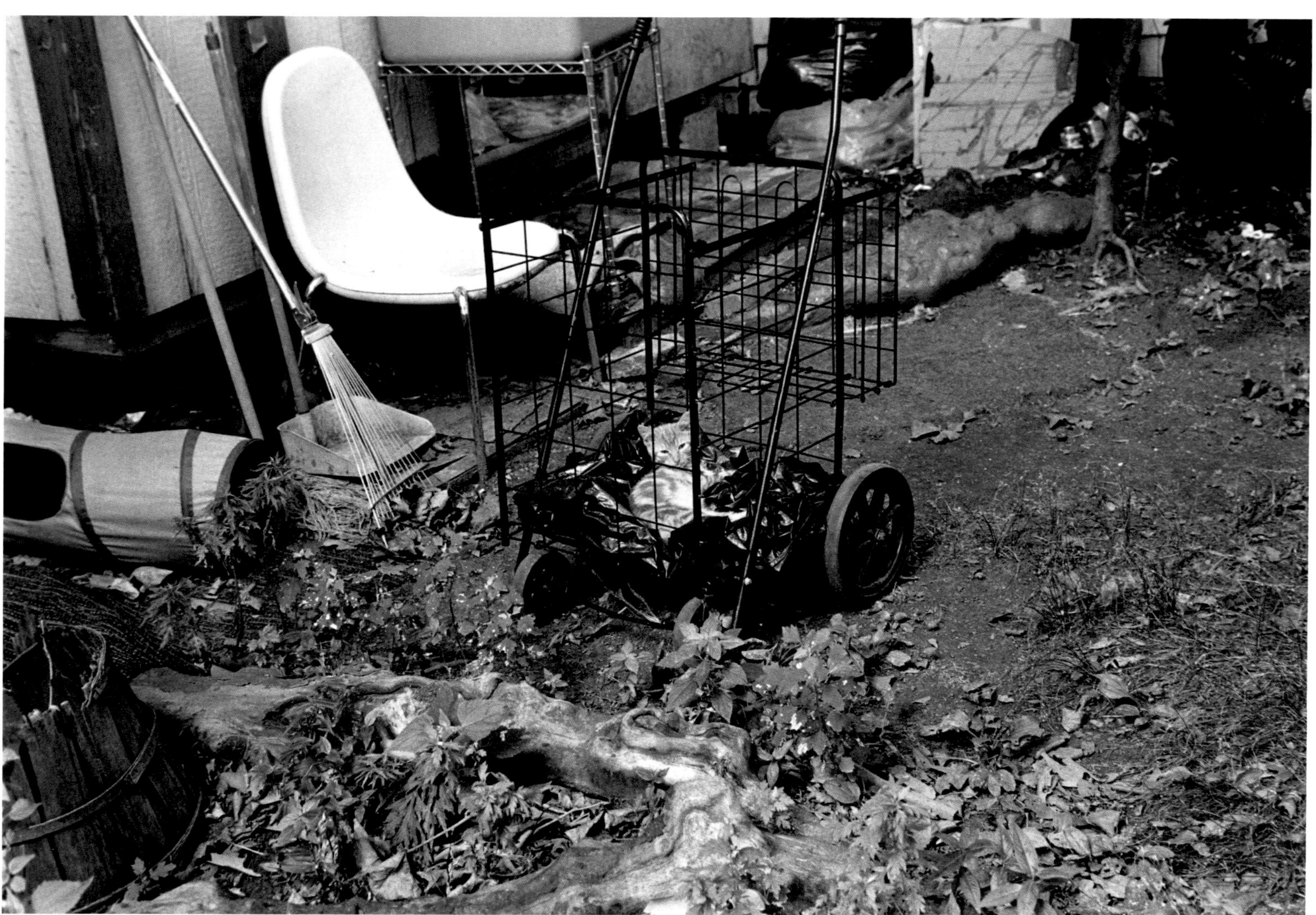

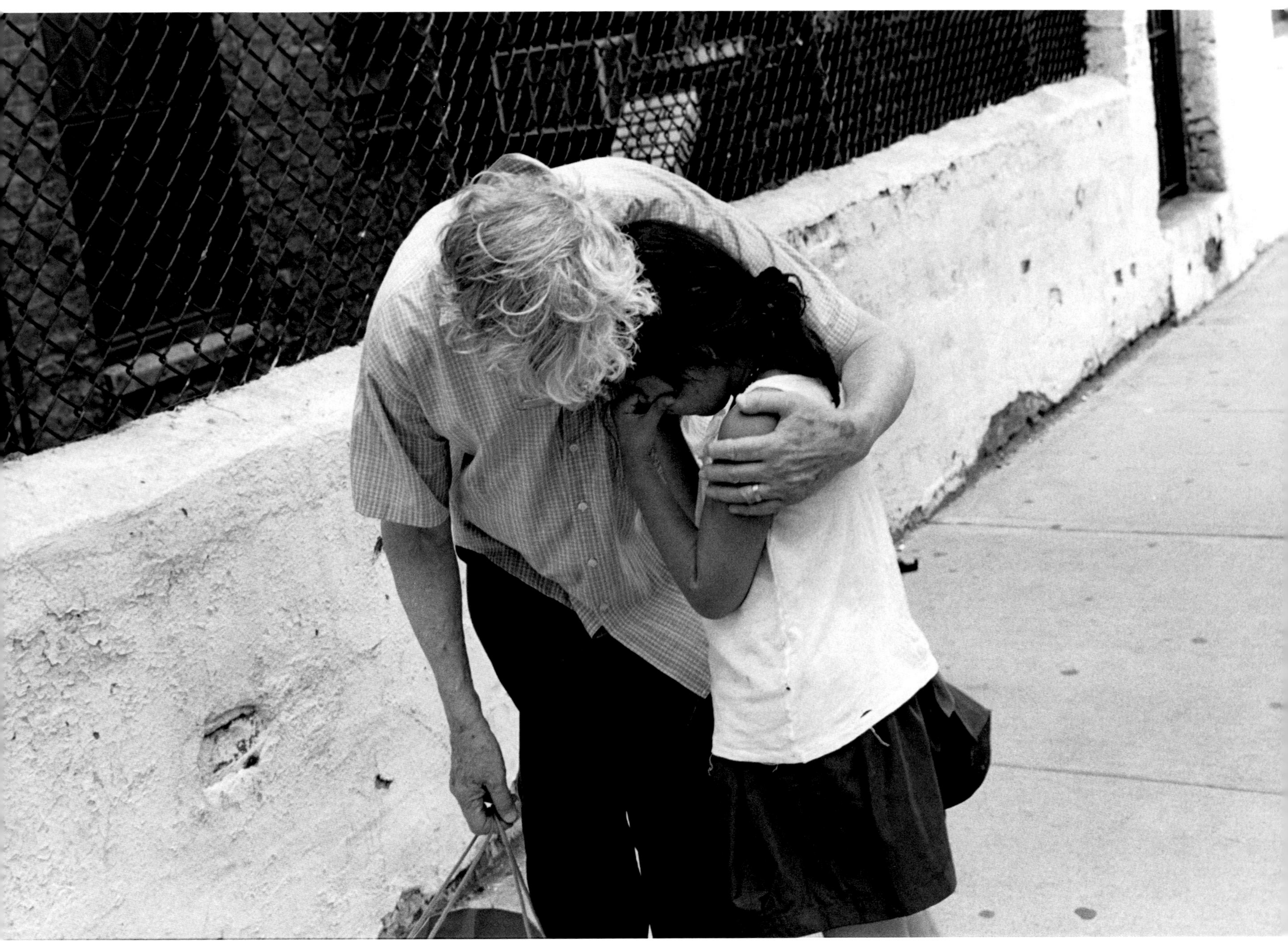

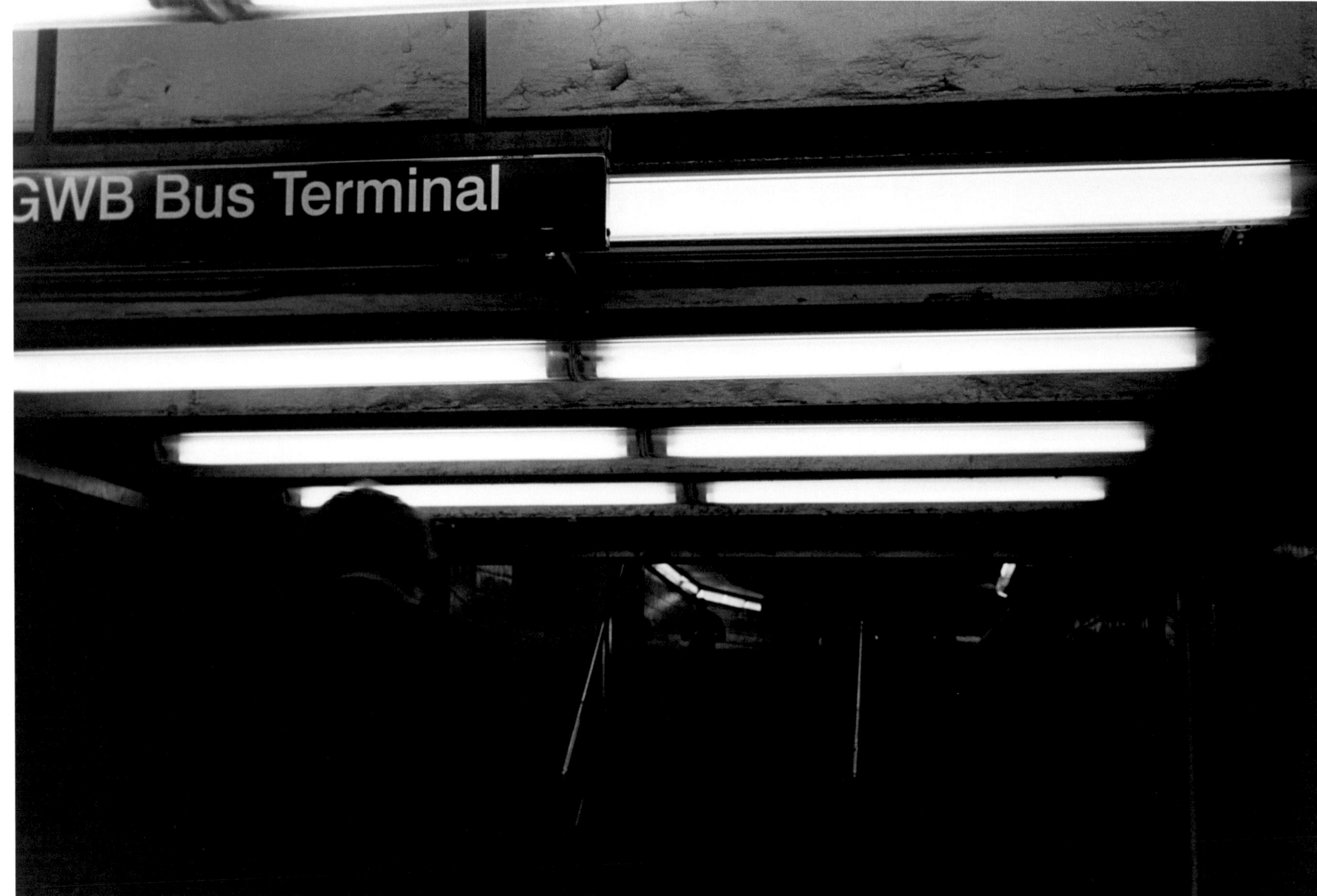

GWB Bus Terminal

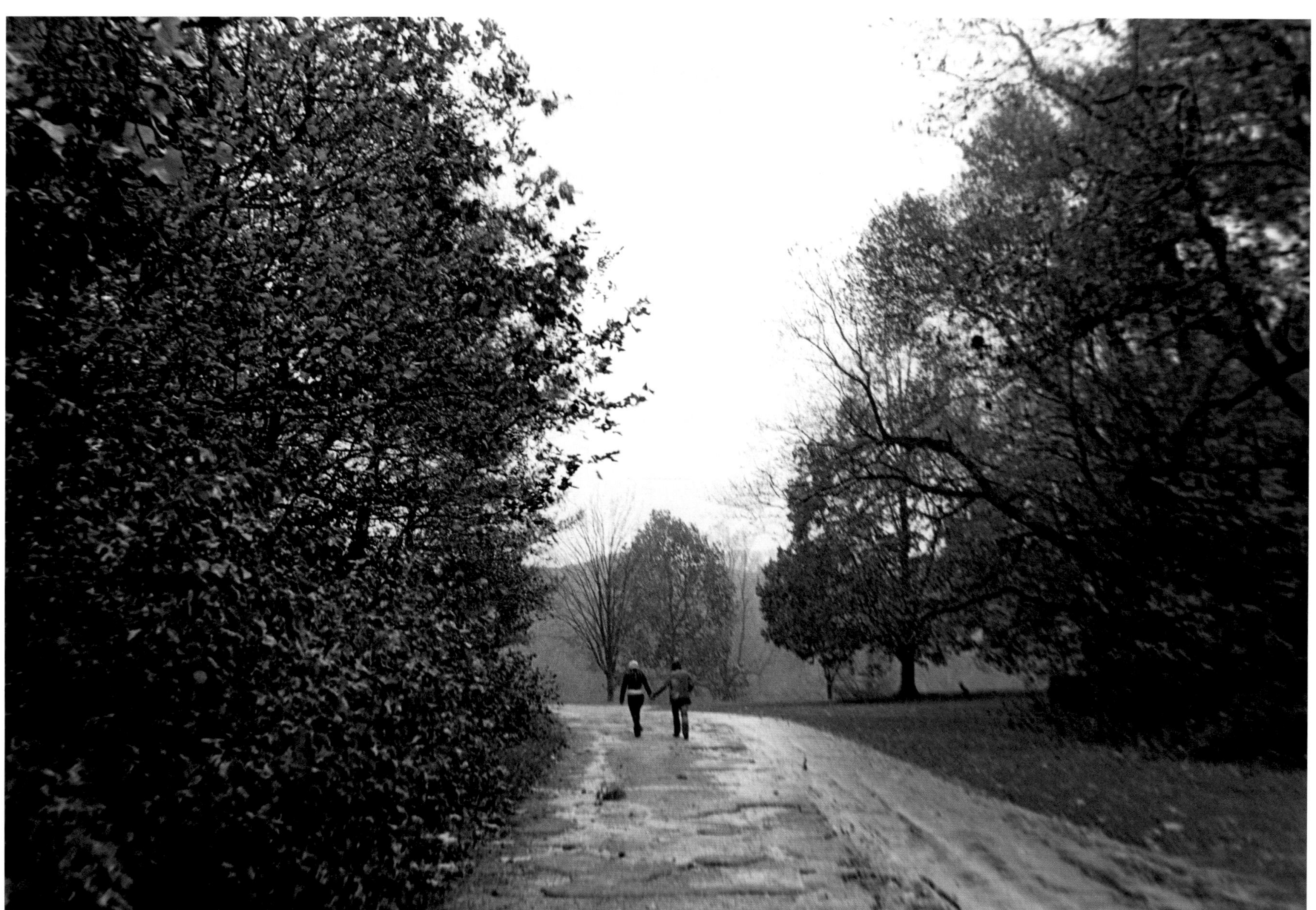

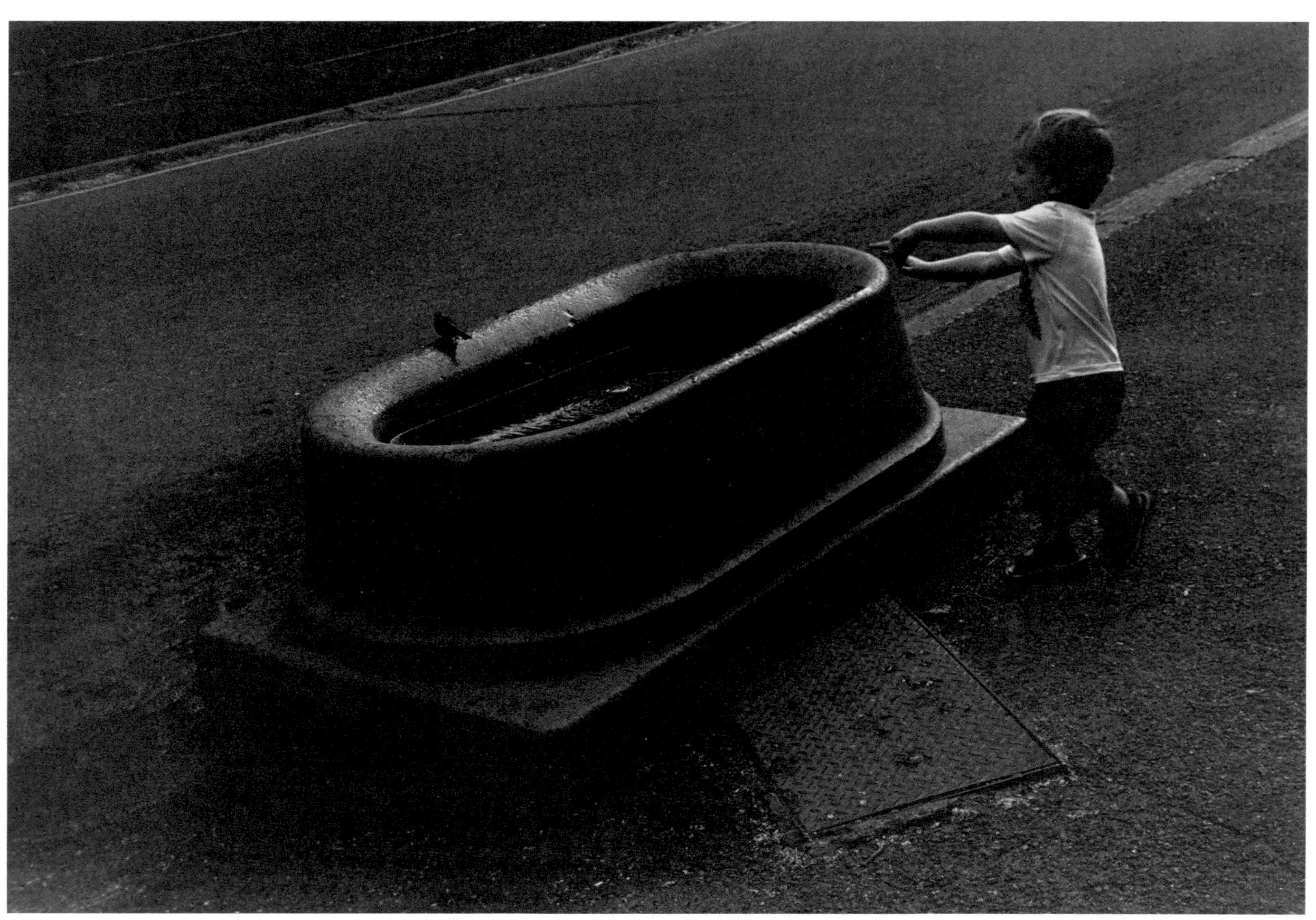

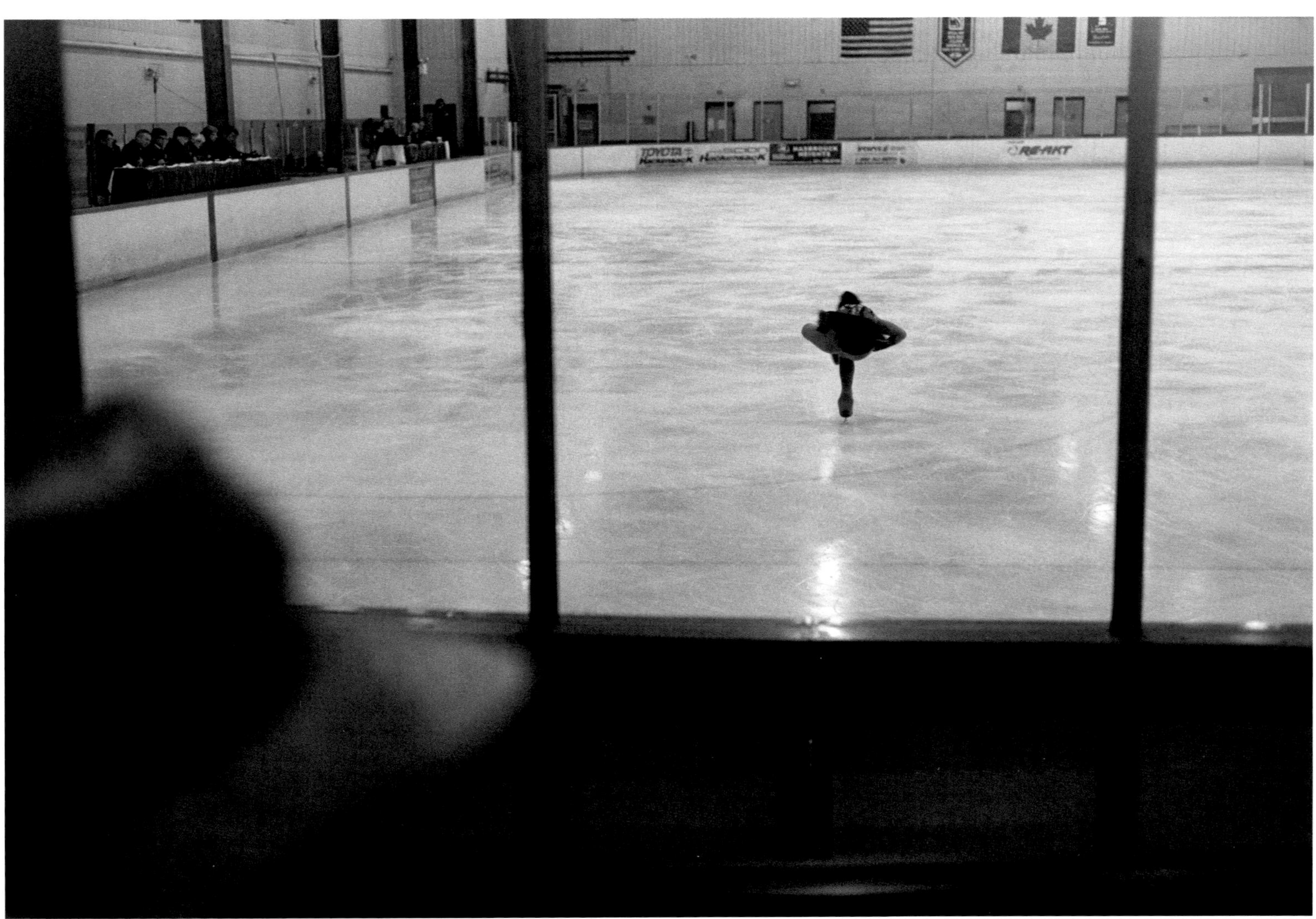

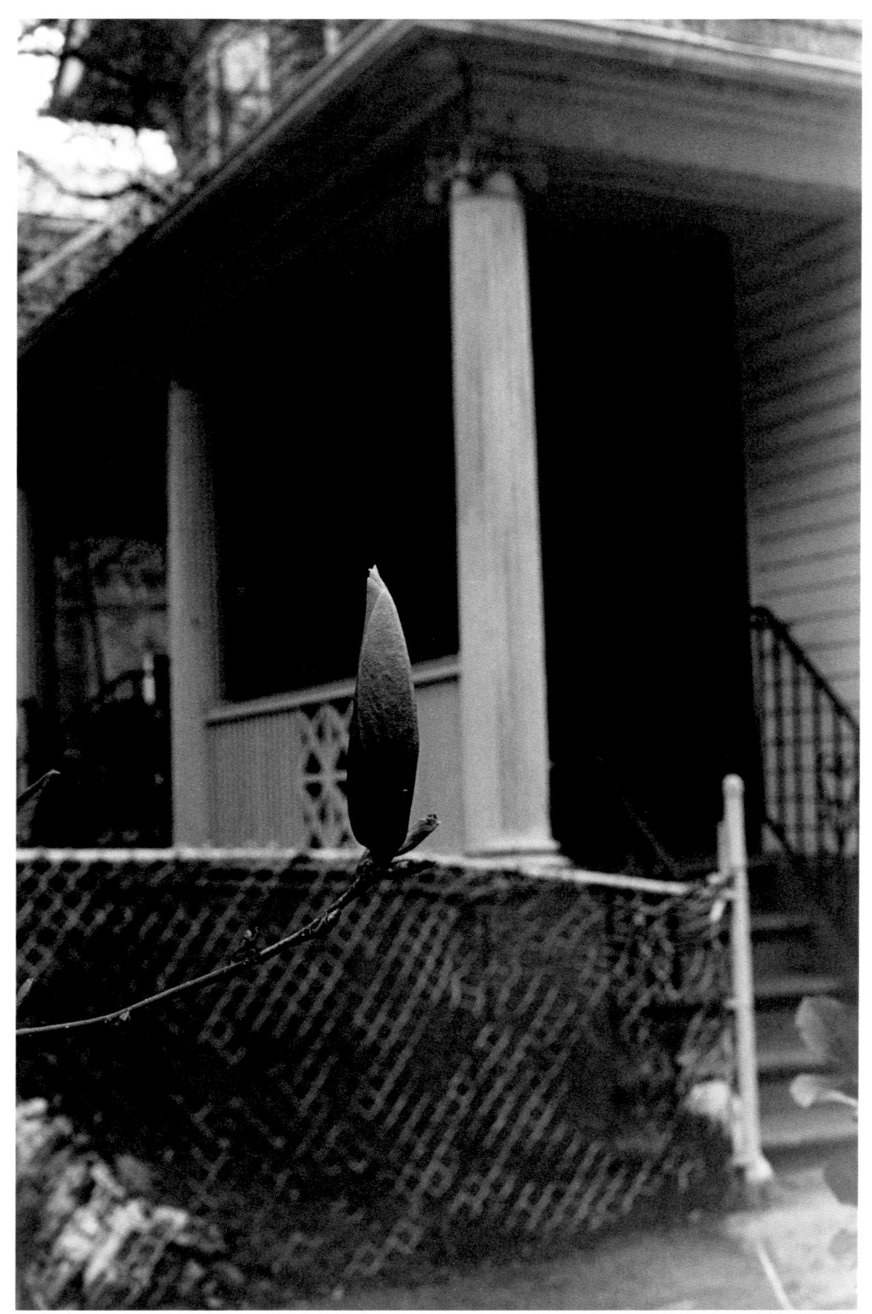

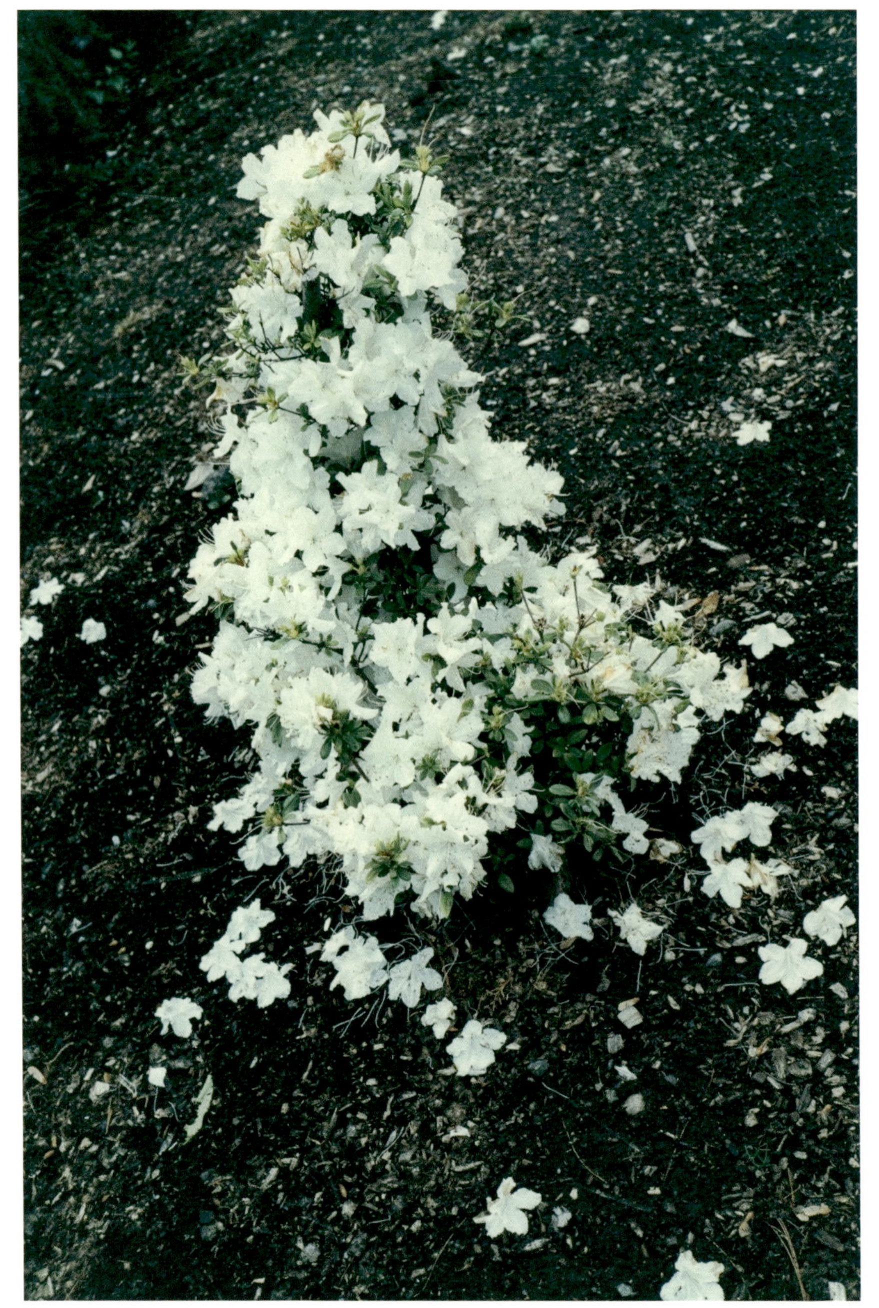

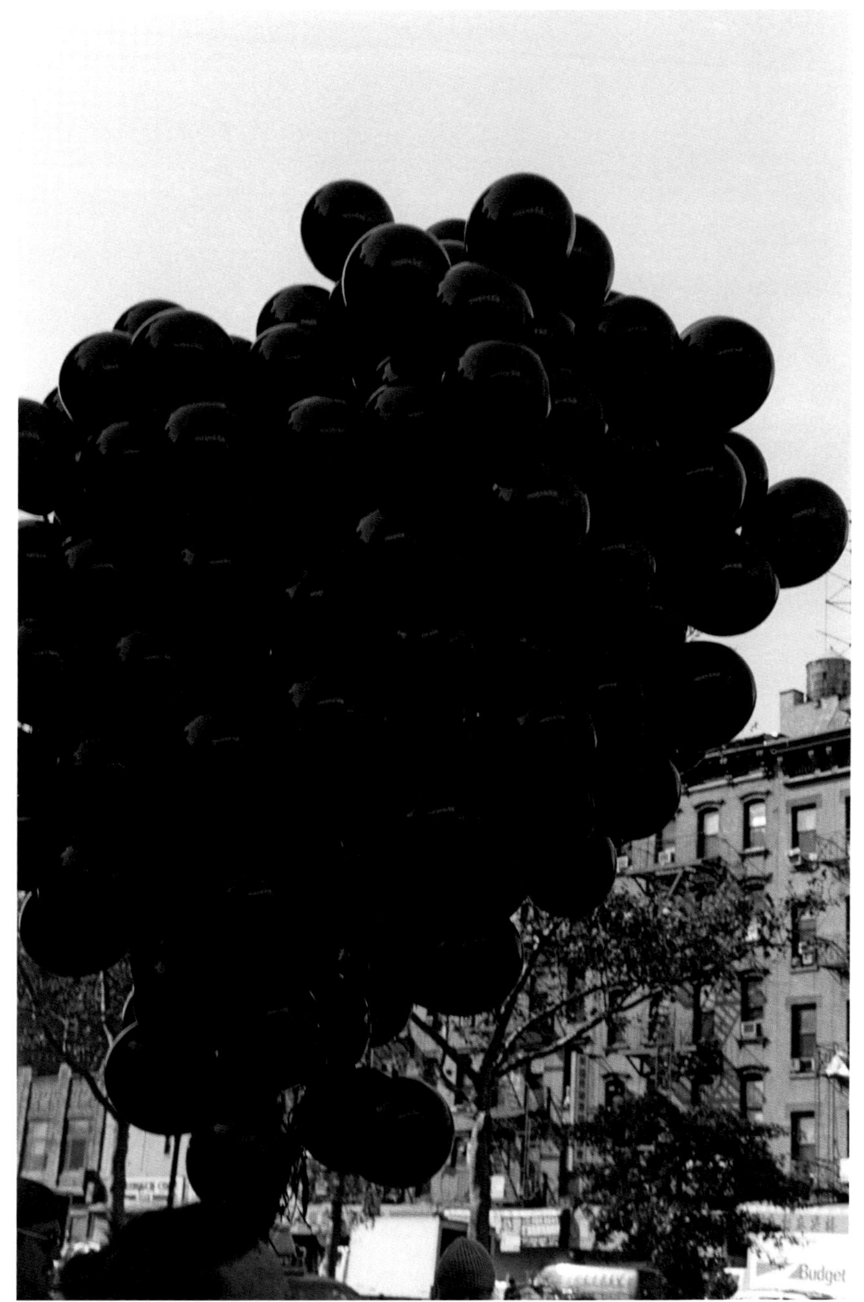

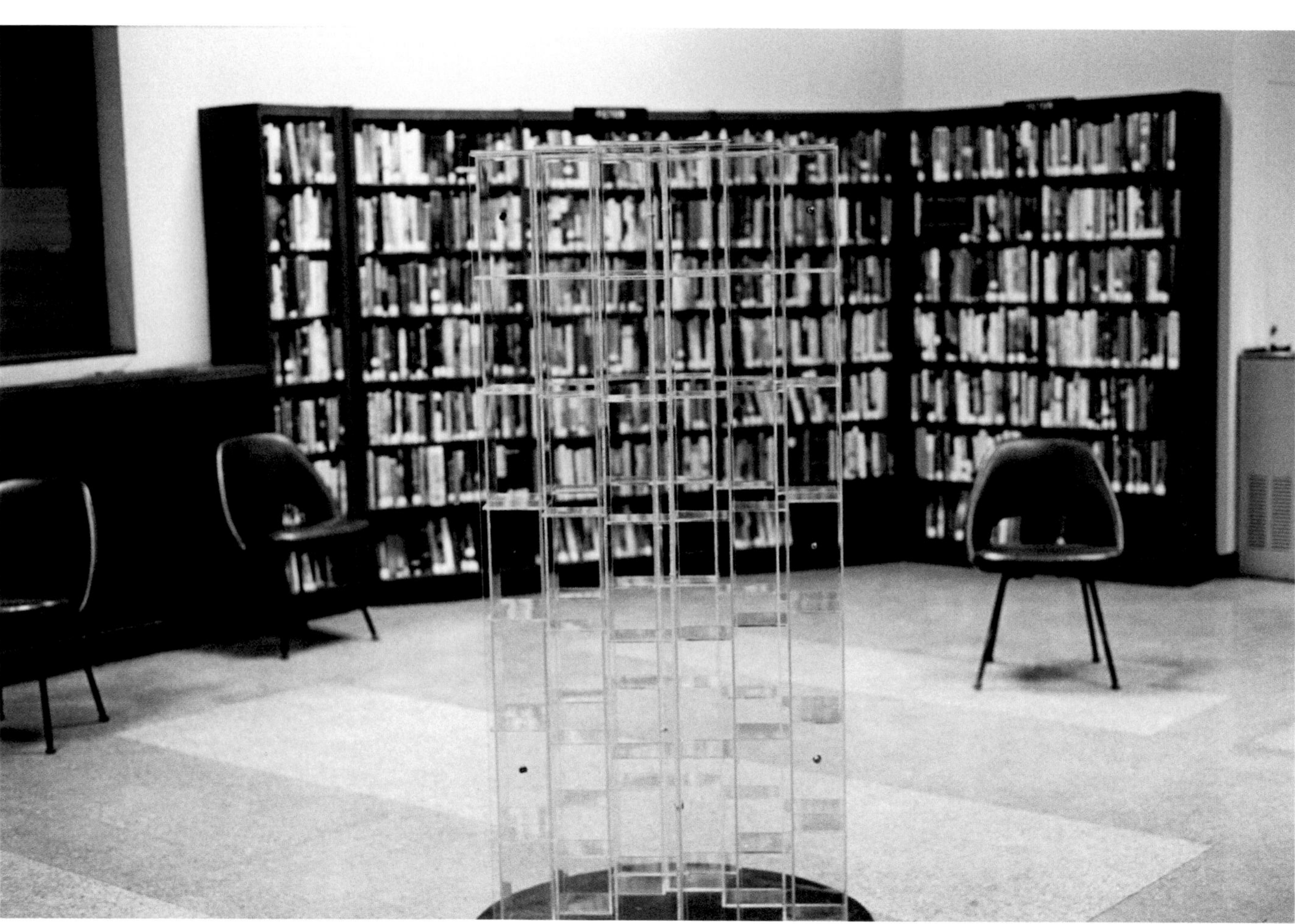

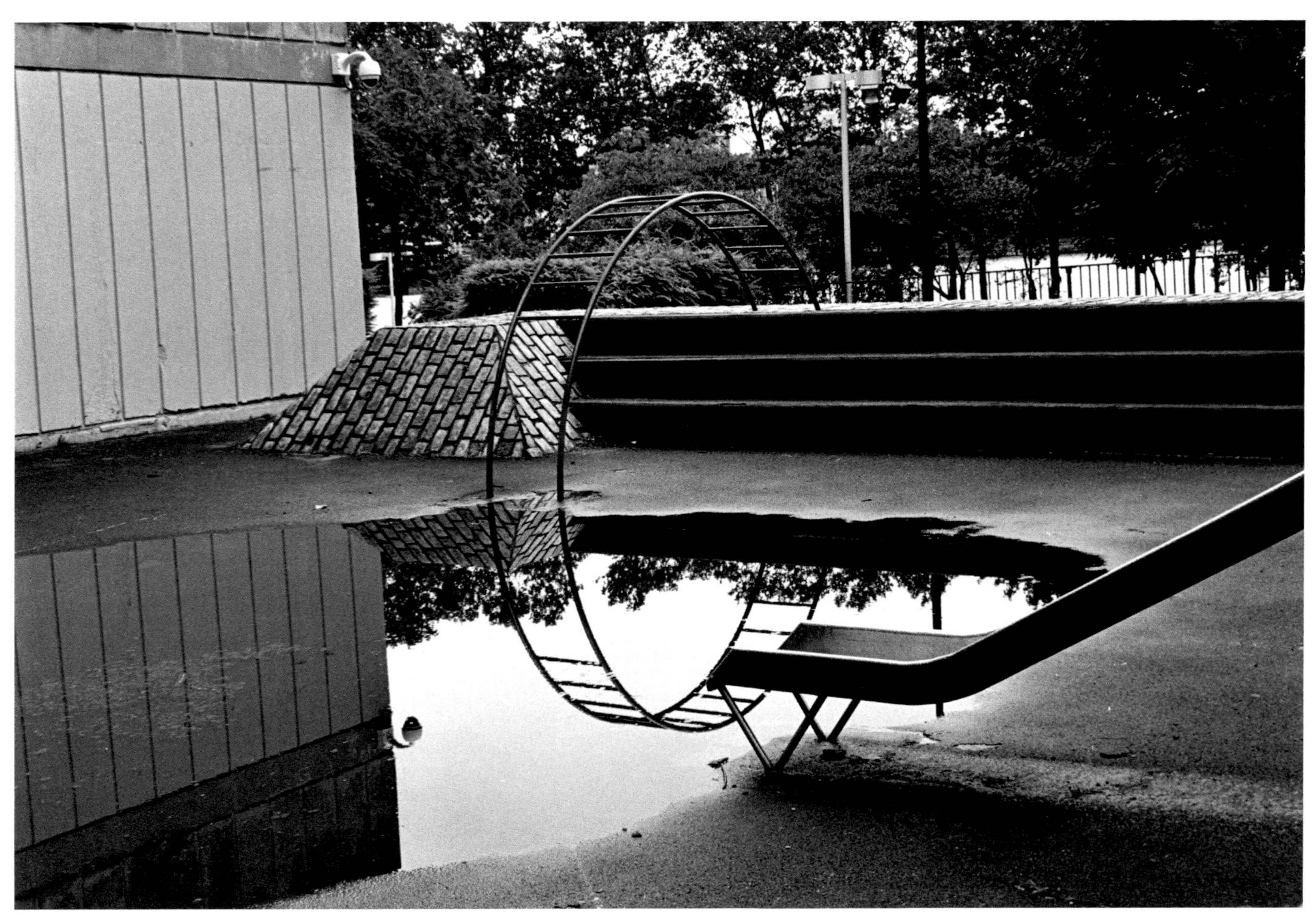

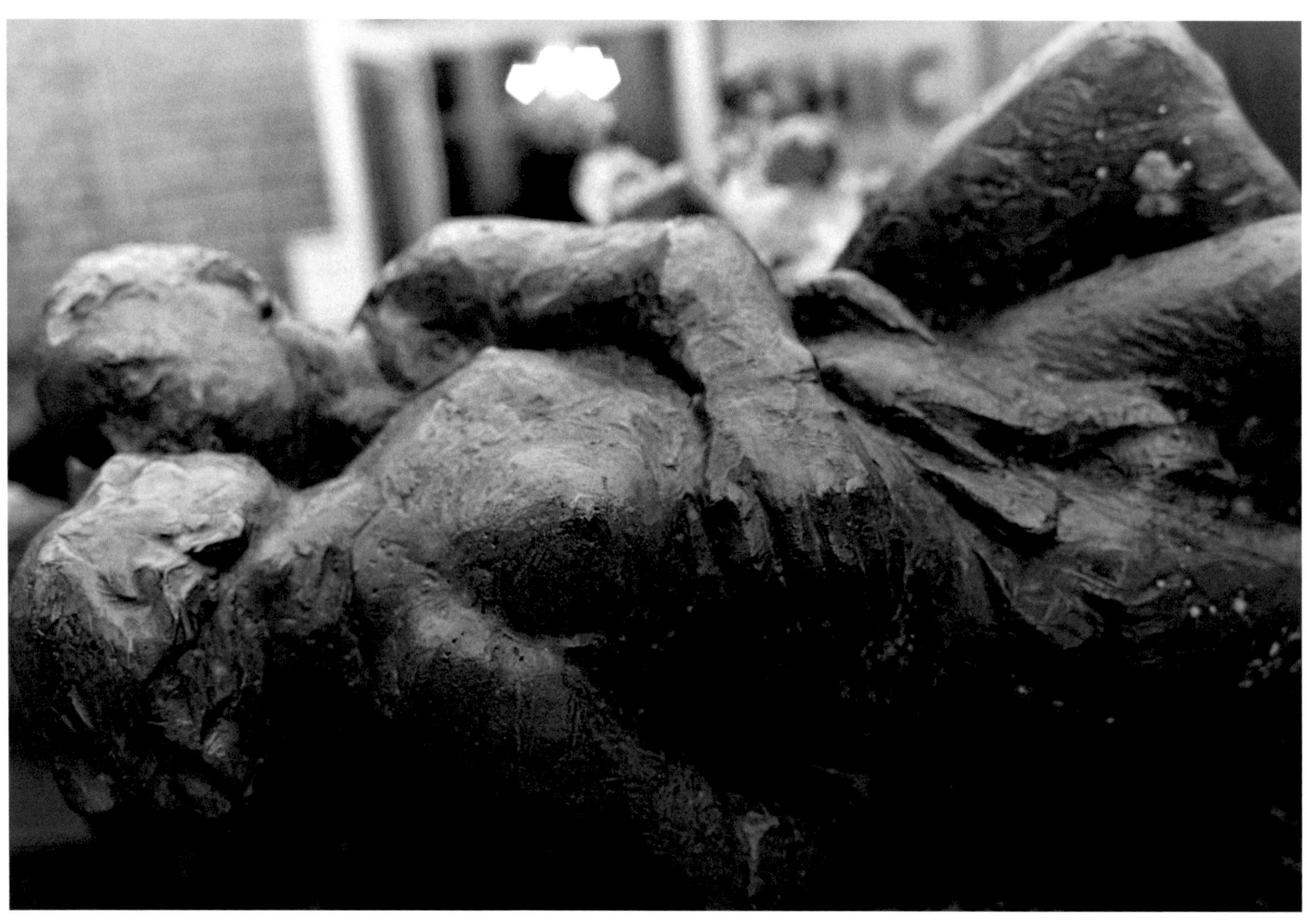

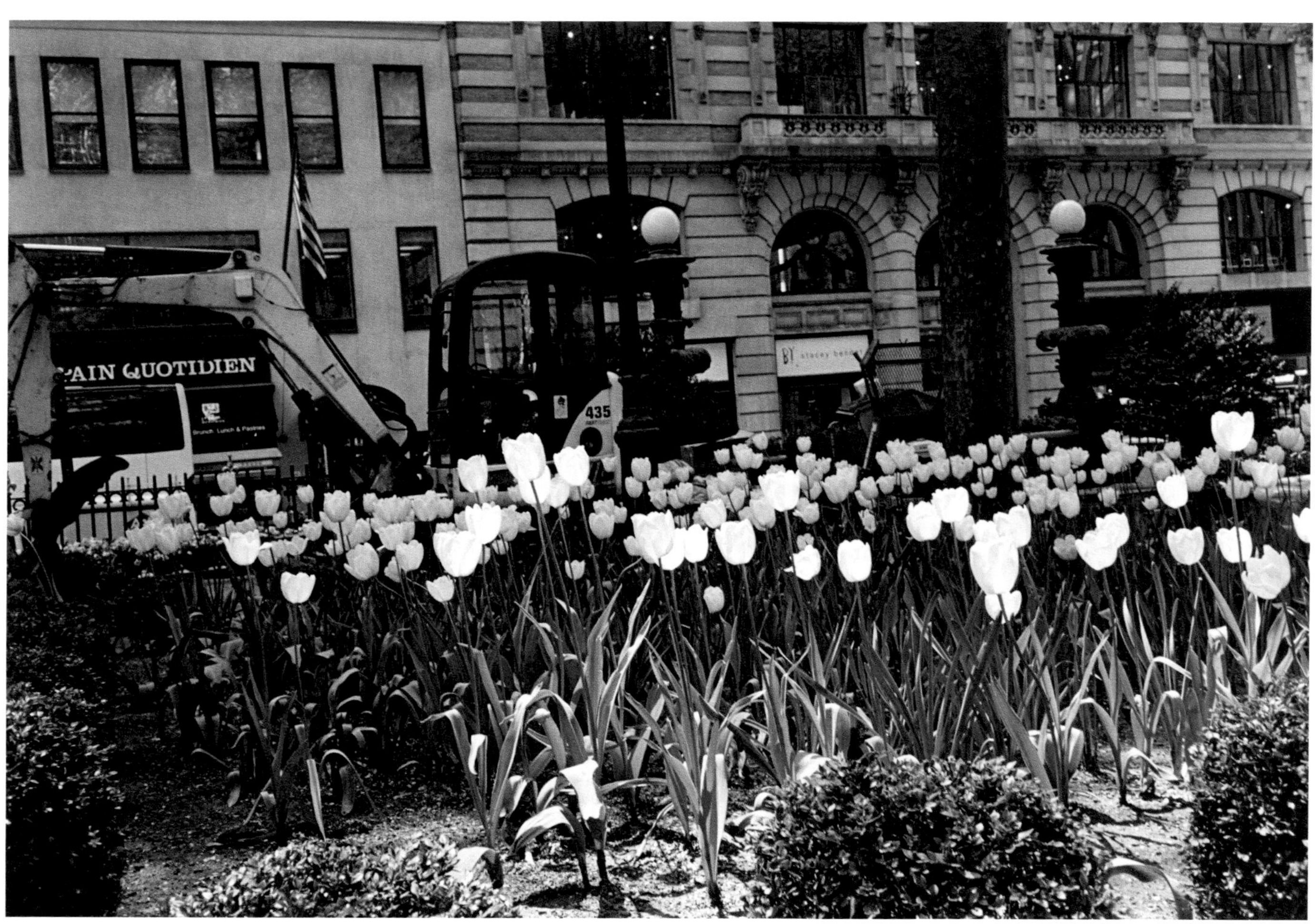
PAIN QUOTIDIEN
Brunch, Lunch & Pastries
435
BY stacey

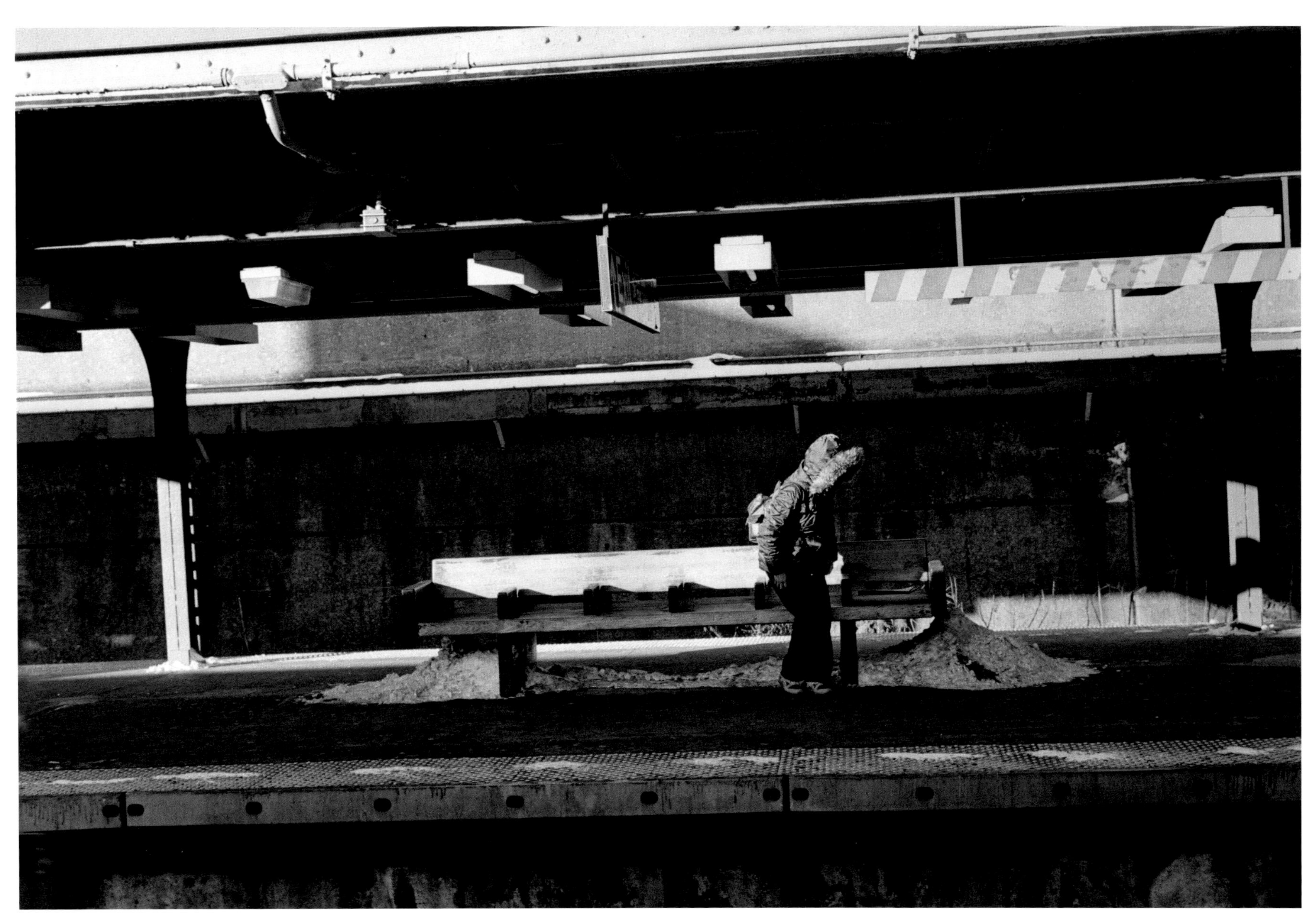

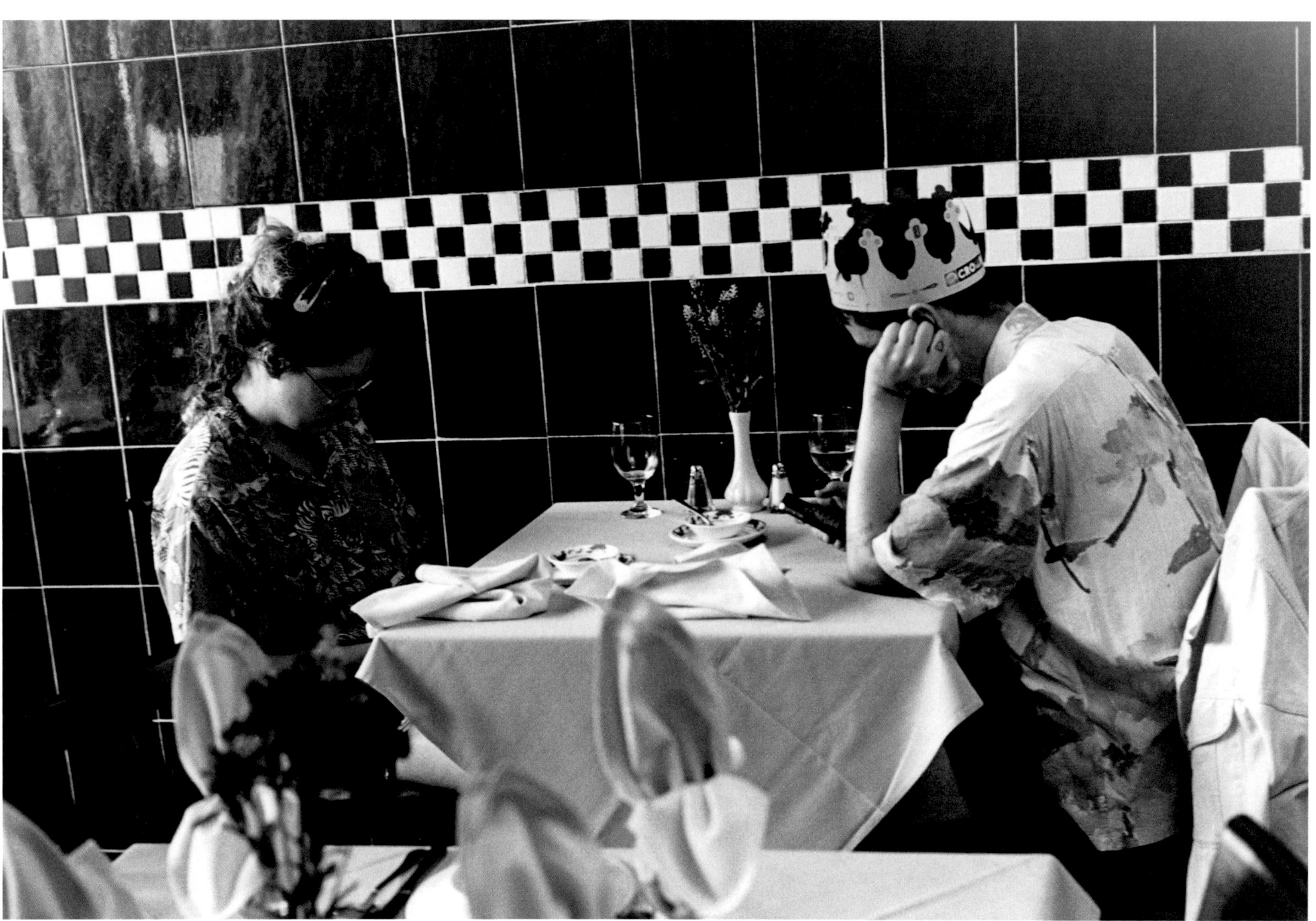

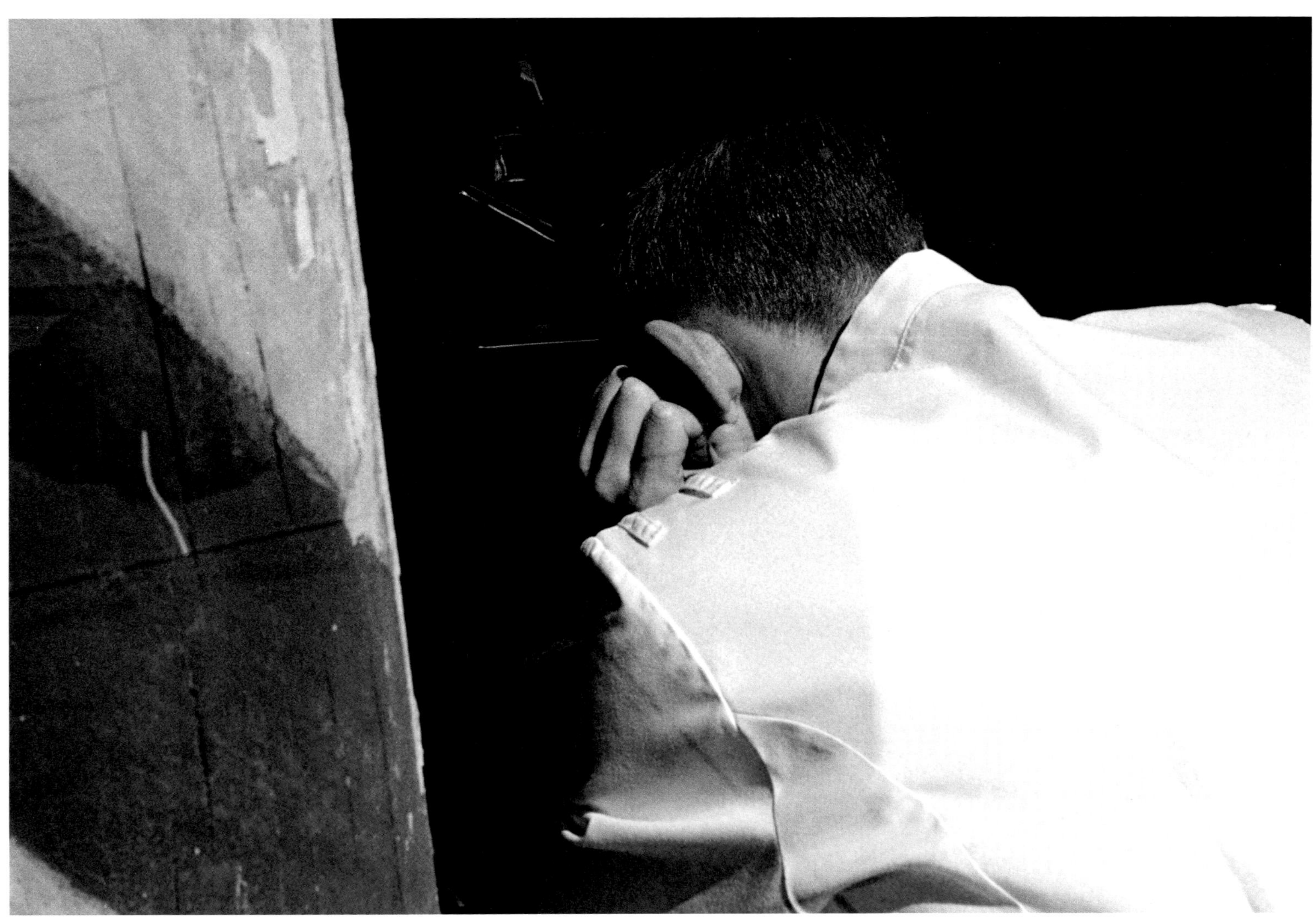

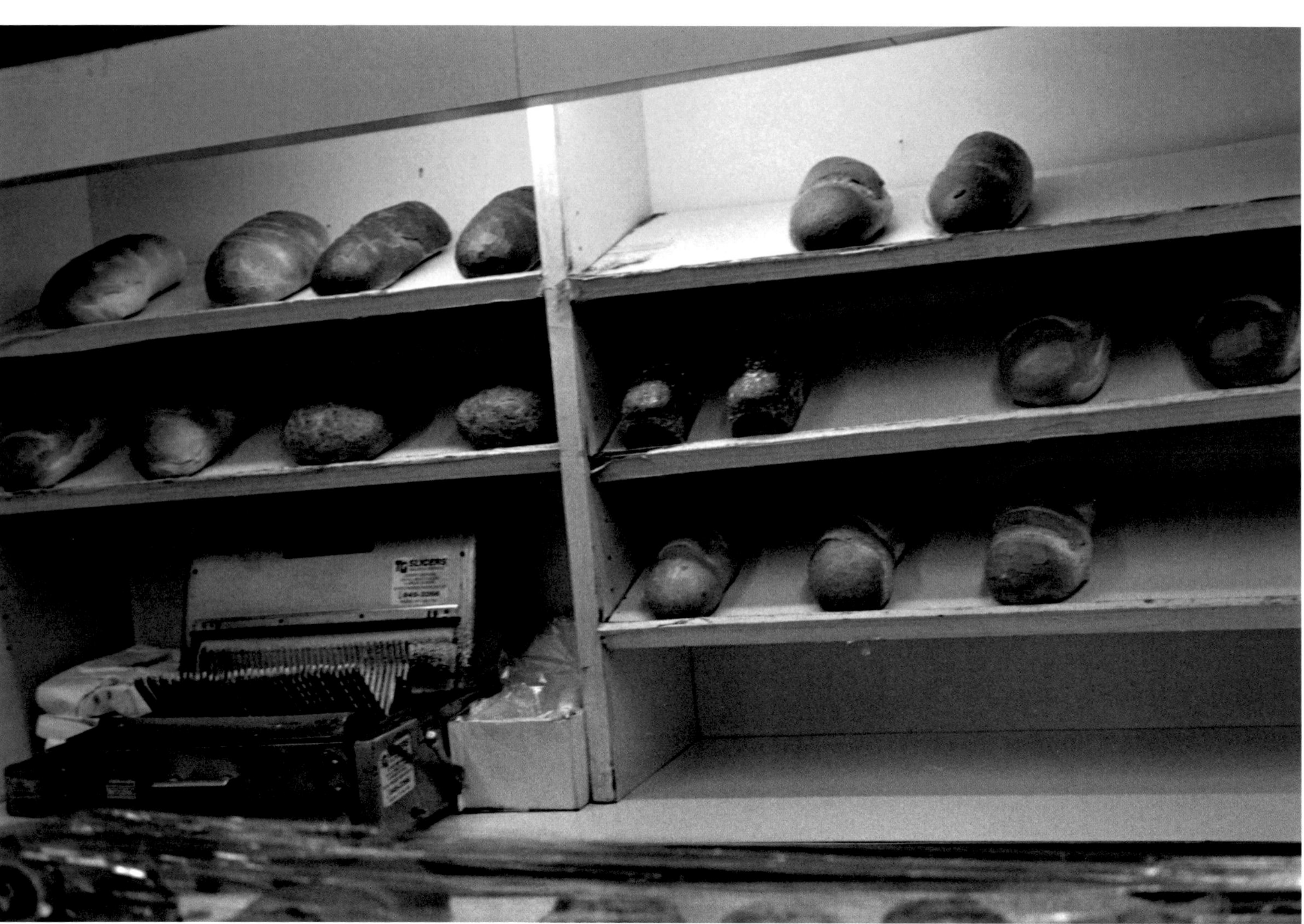

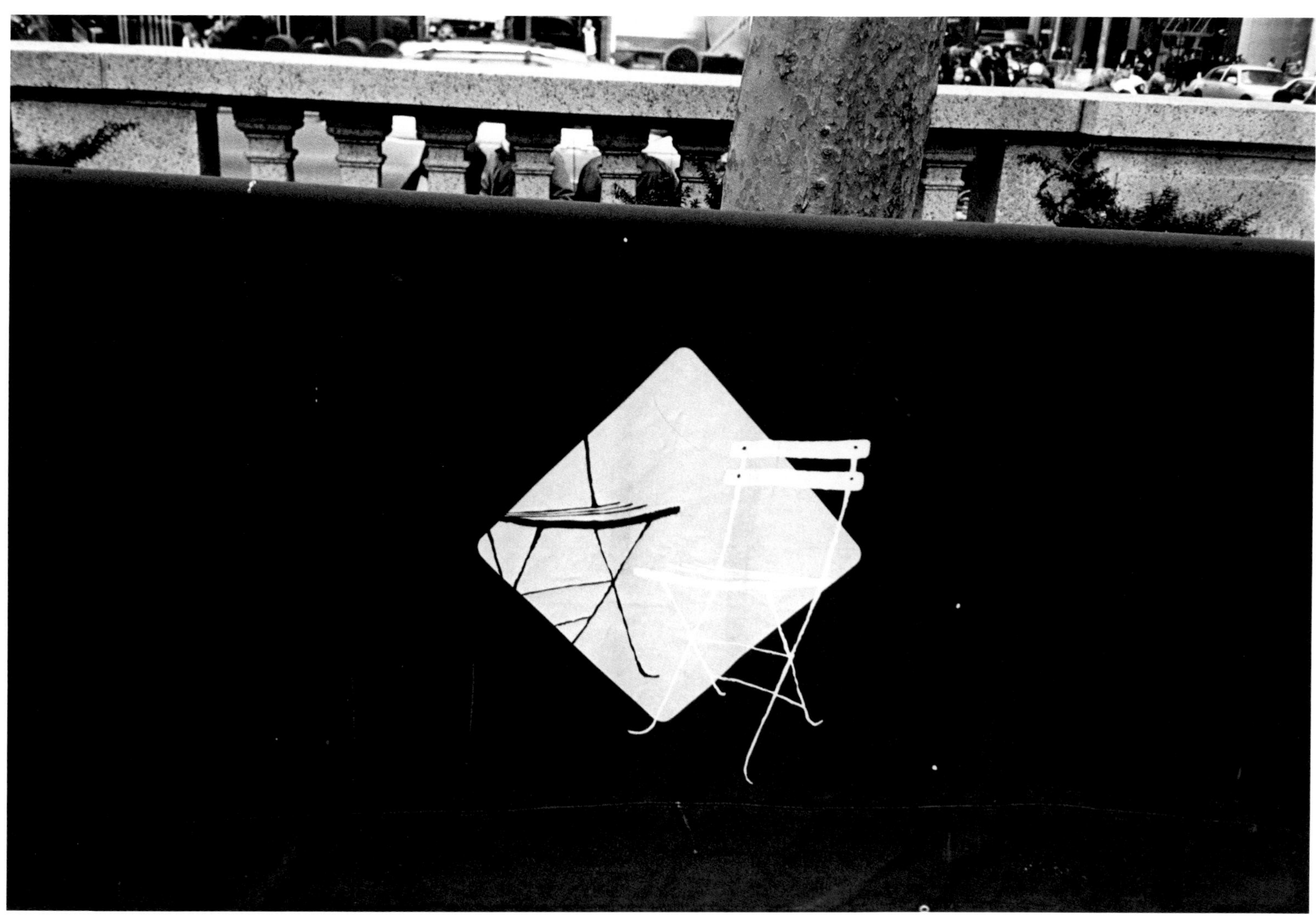

I live near a big park

There is a botanical garden and a small zoo.

The fact that I could see sea lions in 10 minutes

of walking makes me feel easier for whatever it is.

Especially before falling asleep

I see Trees, Algae-covered lake and people BBQing

Season is changing

old man lives with a lot of cats in my Back yard.

I see the kitties playing under the winter sun from a

kitchen window.

They are born a few times a year, only the tough ones servive

sometimes I talk with him about his past.

I dont have bad intuition anymore.

2012 ~ 2014

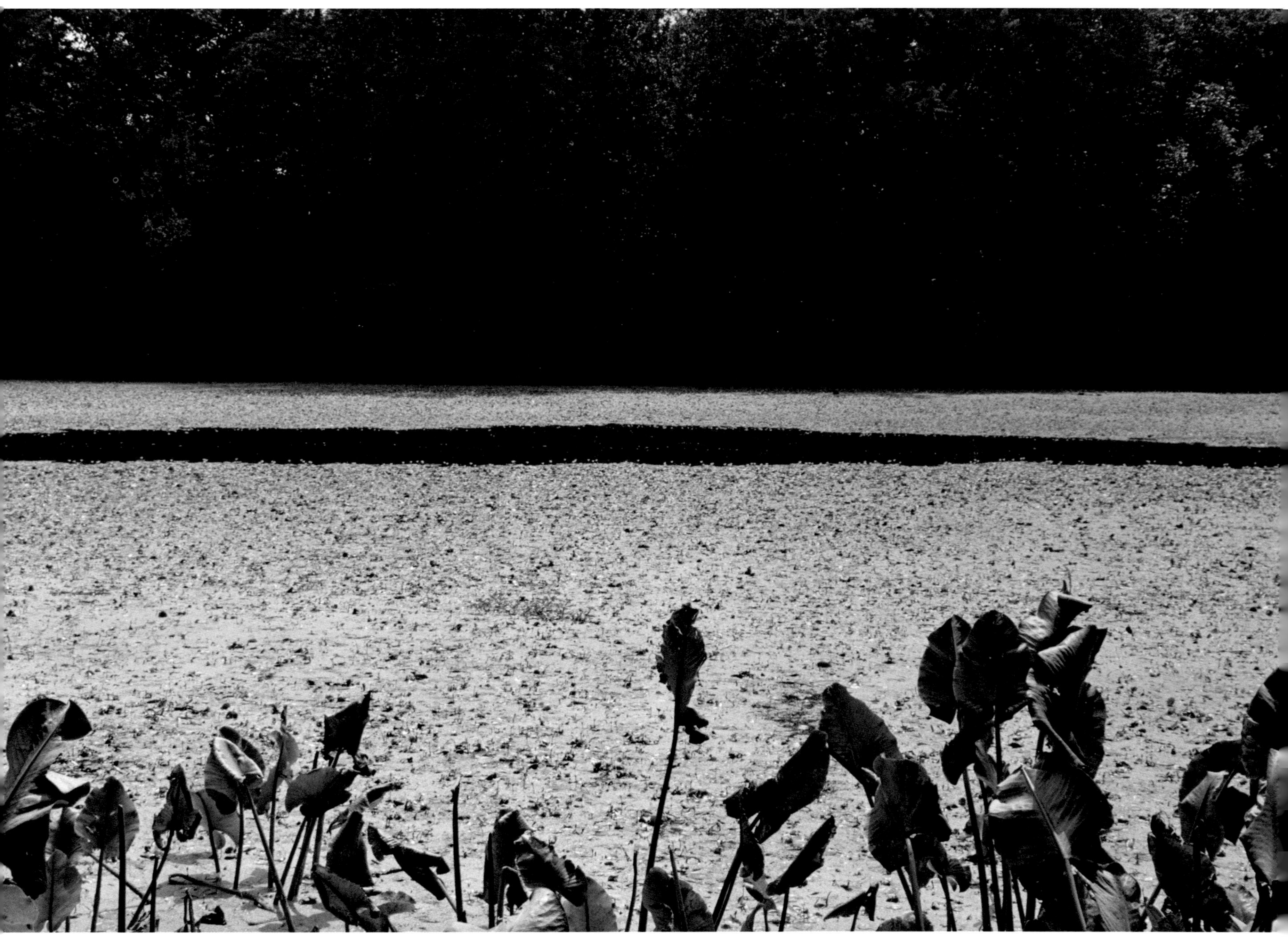

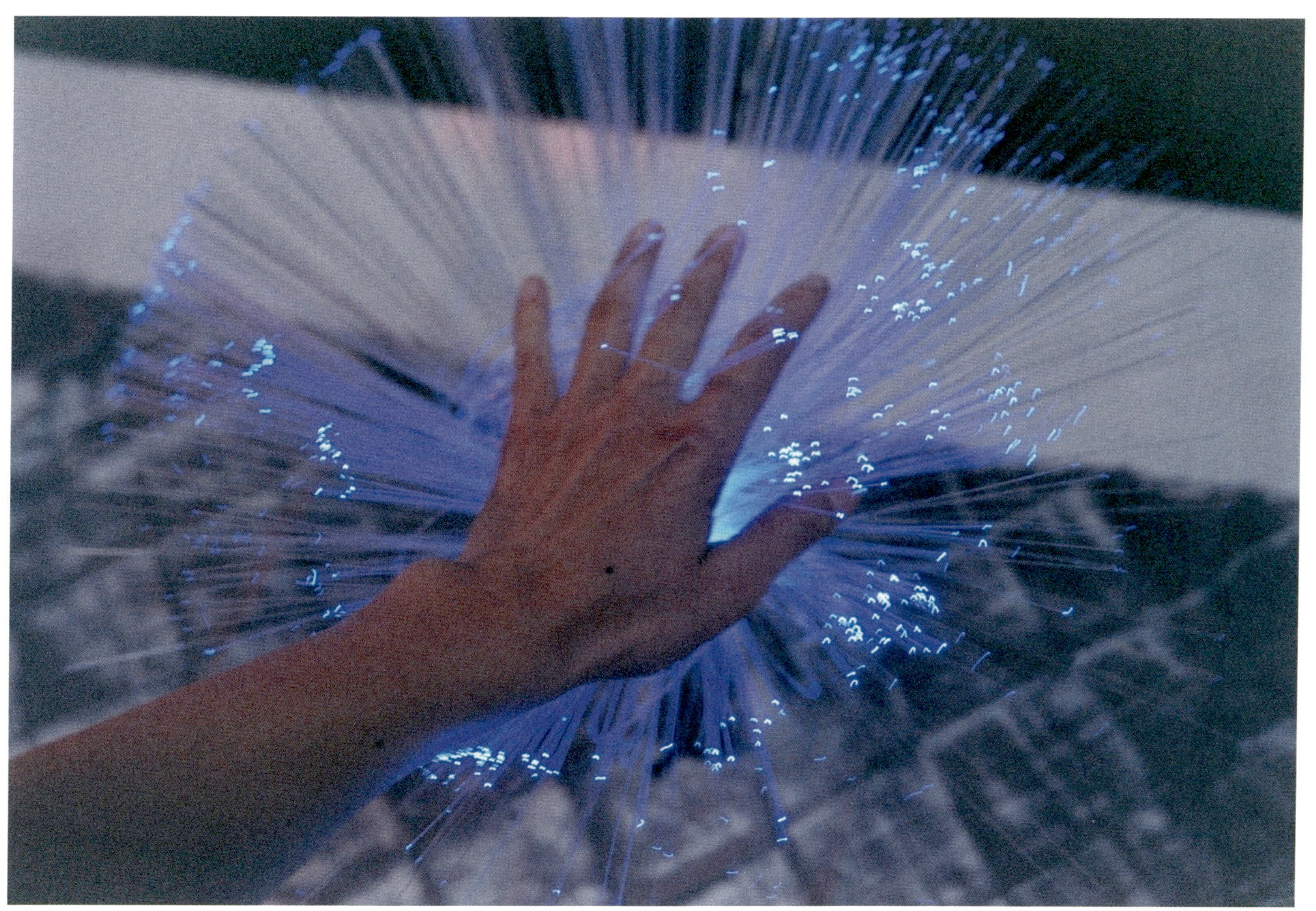

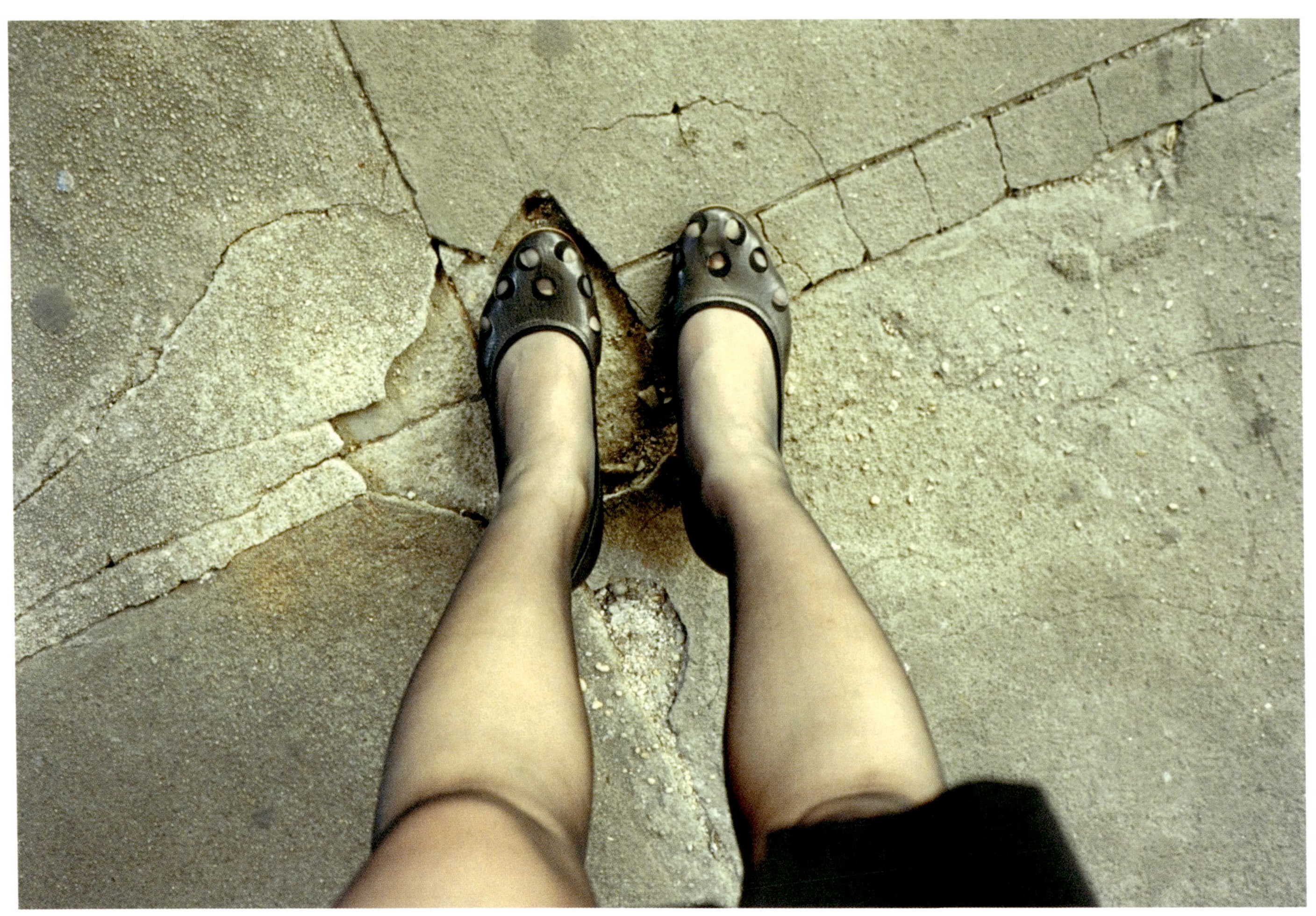

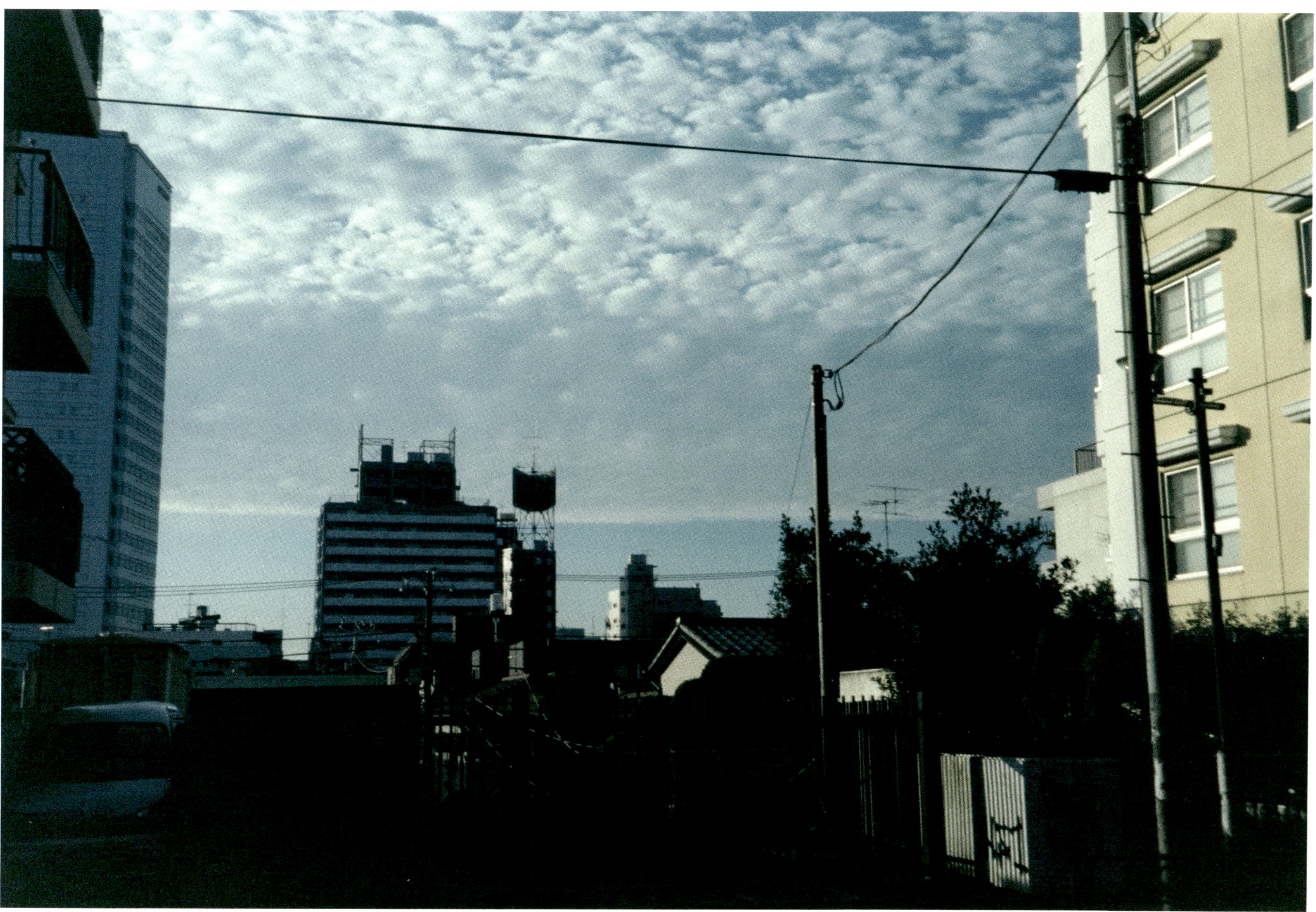

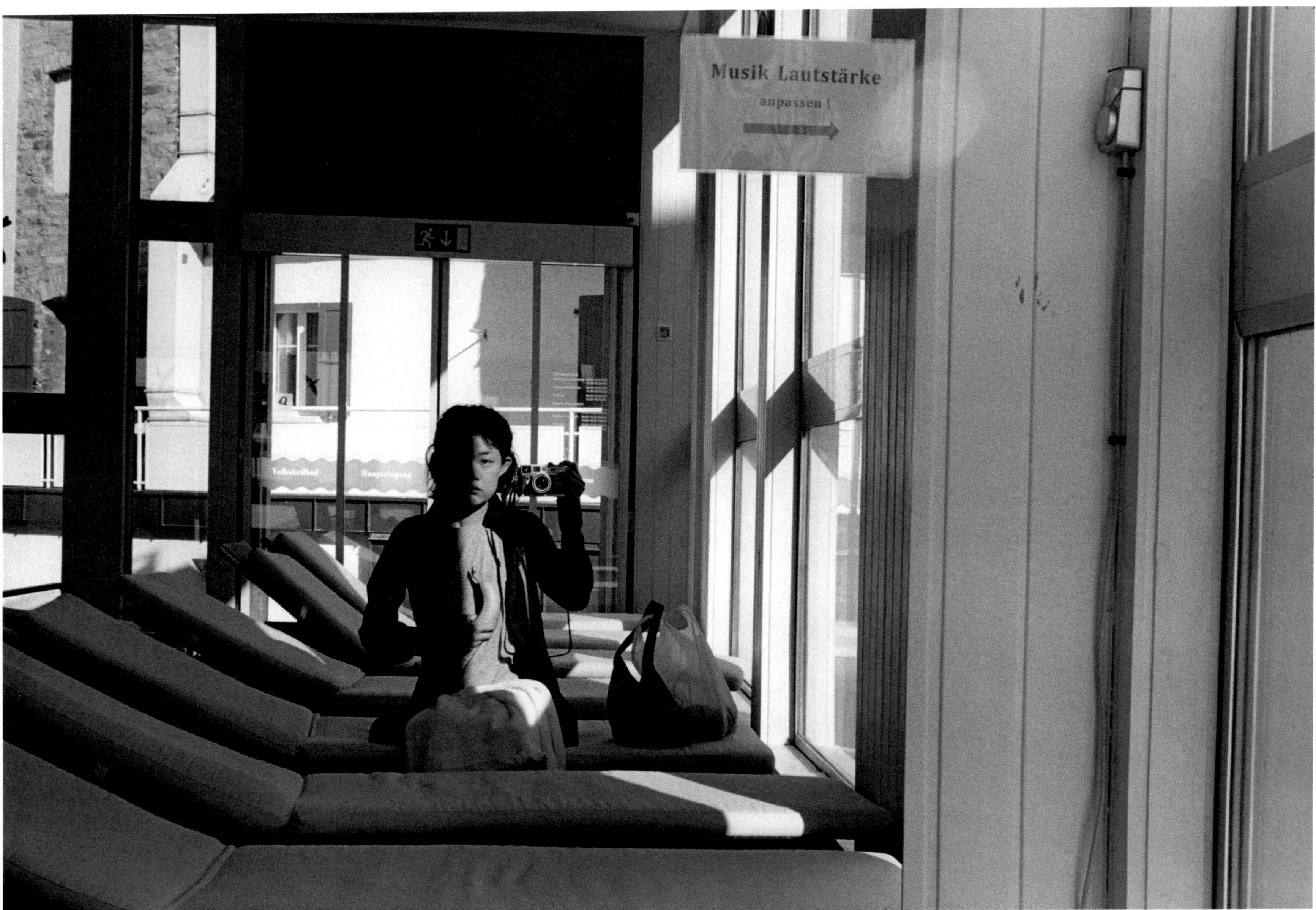

Musik Lautstärke
anpassen !
Volksheilbad    Haupteingang

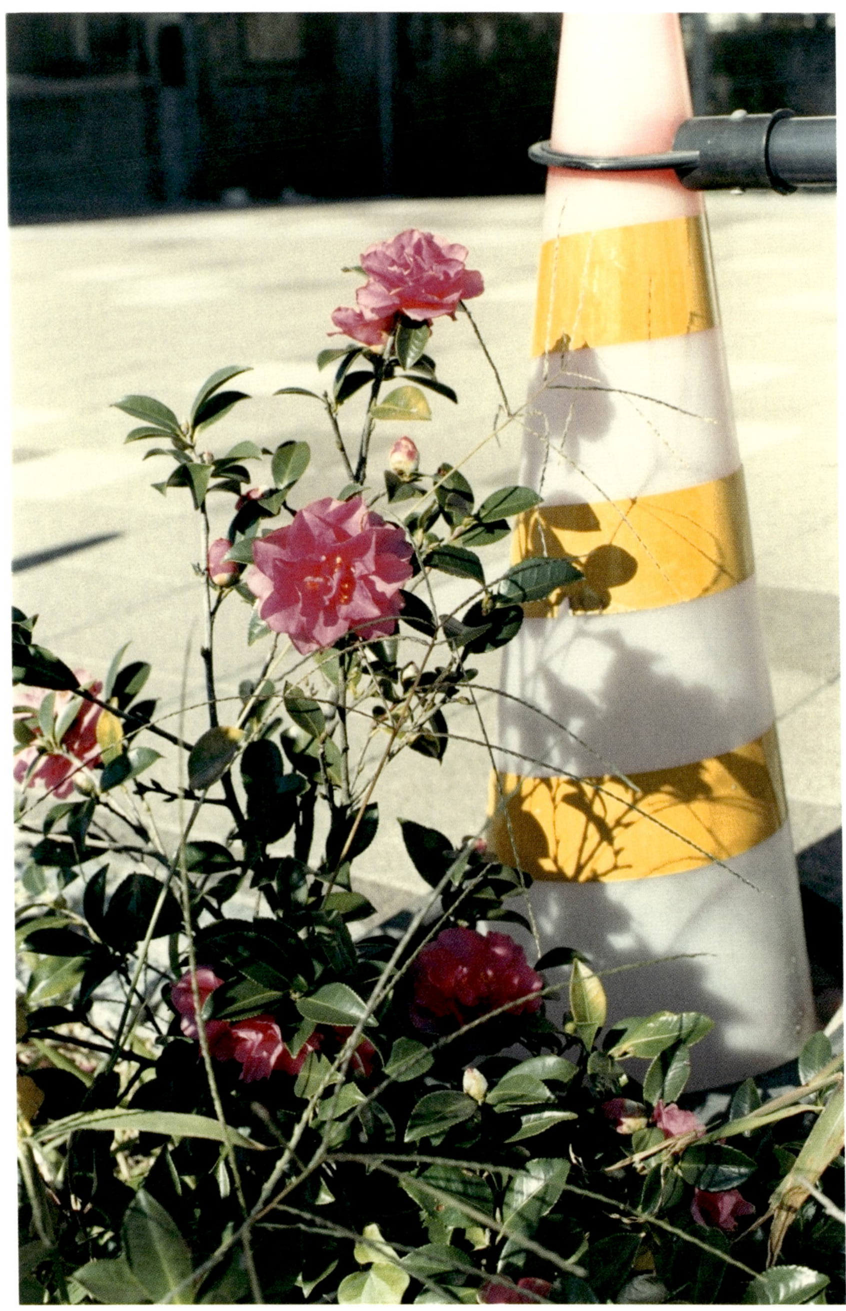

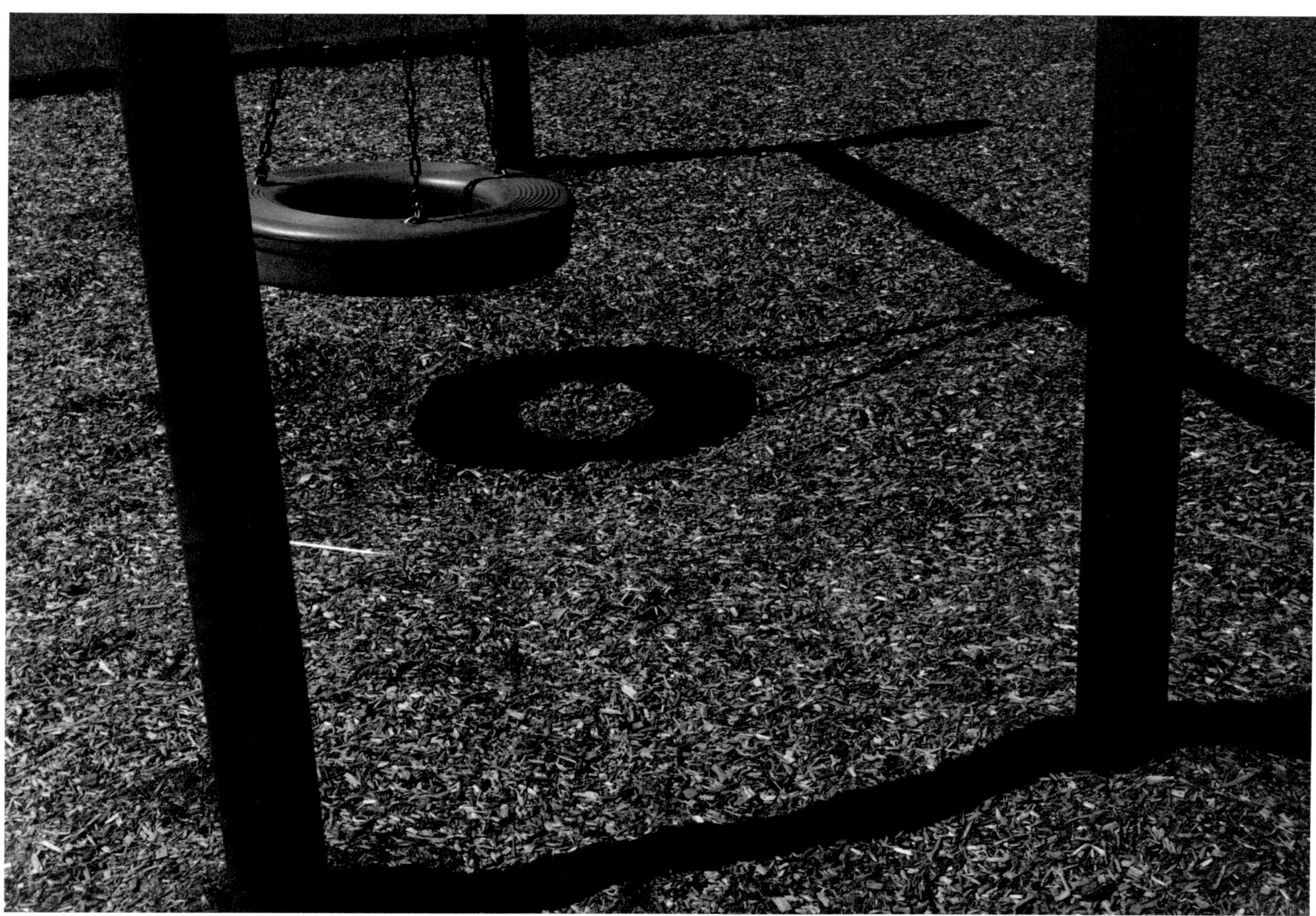

water comes from the faucet

I see a small beauty there as you taught me

meaning less and less everyday

for what was wrong in the air.

That's all left and Enough.

A - CHAN

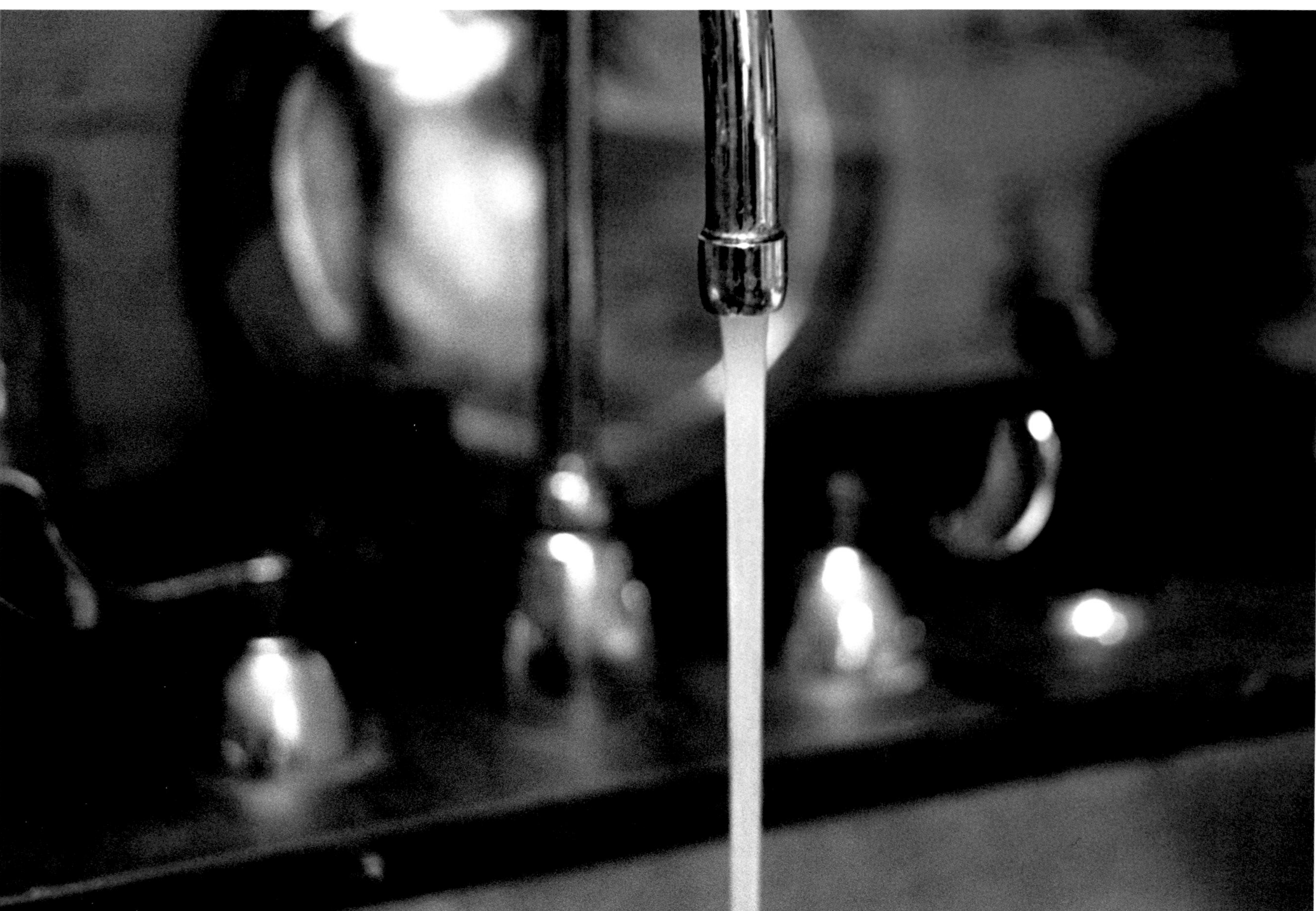

A - CHAN

Salt & Vinegar

published by steidl

© 2016 by A-CHAN

steidl.de

ISBN 978-3-86930-784-8

printed in Germany by steidl